"Lisa Luckett brings an unsparing eye, an open heart, and a survivor's resilience to this deeply personal account of losing her young husband, Ted, on 9/11, and suddenly confronting single parenthood to three children. The aftermath of the worst terrorist attack in modern American history forces her to reckon with long-buried family secrets and the ancestral ghosts who haunted her childhood. What emerges is a master class in self-discovery, acceptance, and the power of love."

—**Kevin Ryan**, author of *Almost Home: Helping Kids Move from Homelessness to Hope*

"Lisa Luckett is a living example that life itself is the most magnificent teacher. Life transformation is available for everyone, even from the darkest hour of our lives. A truly remarkable book of hope and empowerment at a time when humanity, person by person, needs to heal emotional wounds and free ourselves of the numbing grip of fear and move forward into lives of love, joy, and abundance. Lisa says it's easy. Just be kind and let kindness be."

—**Trude Dybendahl**, Olympic medalist, author, speaker, and life coach, Norway

"This book captures the roller coaster ride of emotions when enduring a traumatic loss. Lisa Luckett takes us on a journey of shock, confusion, pain, and creativity into the light. Her honesty, authenticity, and tenacity are expressed and readers will certainly find a piece of themselves in this book. Most importantly, everyone will find answers for the aches they encounter along the journey of life. This book is brilliant, powerful, and spot on! A must read!"

—**Sister Jenna**, Director, Brahma Kamaris, Washington, DC, Host of American Meditating Radio

"This BEAUTIFULLY written book provides the reader and the greater world with vital information to consider related to how one heals the space within oneself—even in the horrific space of trauma, disaster, terrorism, and death. This book showcases the strength we all have hiding beneath our fears and worst nightmares. Lisa Luckett has provided the world with a great gift—to remember that no matter what is going on in our external world—we are never alone. Ultimately—that we are here to help one another with our compassion, our love, and our kindness. This book made me cry, laugh-out-loud and truly reflect on the beauty of humanity and the real meaning of life by remembering that life is the greatest gift and miracle we are all able to share with one another and that love and kindness is, in fact, the light that heals us from the inside out."

—**Paul Luftenegger**, International singer/songwriter/composer, *Faith, Miracle of You, Love Expanding Love*, and other albums.

"Lisa's words moved through me viscerally as my eyes filled with tears. This gem speaks secrets to the heart, which longs for connection, nurturing, safety, and understanding. When you read Lisa's book, chances are you will find the courage to share the secret parts of you that you hold unworthy or shameful. That is Lisa's gift. When you read her words you can feel yourself in her heart.

This book is certainly a journey of love. What a gift it is to hold it in your hands."

—**Karena Virginia**, coauthor of *Essential Kundalini Yoga*, spiritual mentor and life coach

"The message Lisa delivers in this beautiful book is both timely and timeless. 9/11 presented most of us with a specific, harsh wake-up call—no one gets out of life without some loss, pain, or trauma. The book's greatest gift is the reminder that we have free will. We can choose to adopt the victim or 'poor me' mentality or decide that life is happening for us and opt for a more courageous, honest role in our life's journey. Lisa is the epitome of a triumphant hero, accepting the painful lessons of life with grace and passing on the wisdom and hope she discovered to the rest of the world."

—**Andrea Pennington**, MD, C.Ac, author of *I Love You, Me! My Journey of Overcoming Depression and Finding Real Self Love*

"Lisa Luckett faced down the perfect storm and every woman's idea of hell—losing her husband in 9/11, raising three small children alone, a breast cancer diagnosis, and challenging family factors. *The Light in 9/11* is a story of a brave woman who found the strength to carry on and allow the light in these challenges—the silver lining—to shine through and enrich her life, and her children's lives. This book is an inspiration to anyone needing an example of how to rise above their hardships and find their personal power."

—**Margaret Placentra Johnston**, OD, author of *Faith Beyond Belief* and *Overcoming Spiritual Myopia: A View toward Peace among the Religions*

"This is the post 9/11 story we've been waiting for. With honesty, insight, and hope, Lisa's writing will inspire you to seize your personal power. Whatever your struggle, you'll see yourself in her journey. I had a front row seat to Lisa's transformation, as her children's school principal. And now, as her friend, I am grateful for all Lisa, and this amazing book, has taught me."

—**Jamie Sussel Turner**, author of *Less Stress Business* and *Less Stress Life*, business coach and speaker.

"We all remember where we were and what we were doing when the twin towers were hit on September 11, 2001. It was a psychic and physical blow to people around the world. But for Lisa Luckett the events of that day were personal. This book describes the day her husband Ted went to work and didn't come back. But this is a book about hope, about love, family, heartbreak, and resilience. It's about how one person can choose hope over despair, and life over endless sorrow. It's a story that will inspire and enlighten anyone who reads it."

—**Bar Scott**, author of *The Present Giver* and singer/song-writer/composer of *Parachute, Grapes and Seeds* and other albums

The
LIGHT
in 9/11

[signature]

xo

"It is of great importance that we bring the message of forgiveness and love to the world."

—EHL

The
LIGHT
in 9/11

Shocked
BY *KINDNESS,*

Healed
BY *LOVE*

LISA LUCKETT

For information about this title or to order other books
and/or electronic media, contact the publisher:

Lisa Luckett
Cozmeena Enlightened Publishing
www.cozmeena.com
info@cozmeena.com

Library of Congress Preassigned Control Number: In progress

ISBN: 978-1-7321971-0-7 soft cover
ISBN: 978-1-7321971-1-4 ebook
ISBN: 978: 1-7321971-2-1 audio

Printed in the United States of America

Cover and Interior design: Peggy Kafka Sackler, Cover Art
1106 Design, Phoenix, AZ

Publisher's Cataloging-In-Publication Data
(Prepared by The Donohue Group, Inc.)
Names: Luckett, Lisa.
Title: The light in 9/11 : shocked by kindness, healed by love / Lisa Luckett.
Other Titles: Light in nine/eleven
Description: [Fairhaven, New Jersey] : Cozmeena Enlightened Living, [2018] | Series:
The light in 9/11 series
Identifiers: ISBN 9781732197107 (softcover) | ISBN 9781732197114 (ebook)
Subjects: LCSH: Luckett, Lisa. | September 11 Terrorist Attacks, 2001--Personal narra-
tives. | Husbands--Death--Psychological aspects. | Life change events--Psychological
aspects. | Kindness. | LCGFT: Personal narratives.
Classification: LCC HV6432.7 .L83 2018 (print) | LCC HV6432.7 (ebook) | DDC
974.71044092--dc23

To the thoughtful friends and strangers, near and far, who gave us their loving kindness and never let us fall.

To the firefighters, police, first responders, and rescue and recovery workers who selflessly gave their lives to help others in the ultimate act of kindness.

And for Jen, Billy, Timmy, and Teddy

TABLE OF CONTENTS

PREFACE

I n the winter of 2016, I saw a commercial for the opening of the Broadway play, *Come from Away*, about the little town in Newfoundland that housed, fed, and supported the 9,000 passengers marooned there when planes were diverted from various airports as a result of the attacks on 9/11.

A glimmer of hope flashed in my mind: Were people finally ready for a positive story about the event that single-handedly changed our world forever? I had been gearing up to talk about my post-9/11 discoveries for years. Now with the opening of the play, it seemed the time had finally come.

Having studied and processed my unique experiences from micro to macro, local to global, personal to general in the years that followed, I had arrived at some uncommon theories and thoughtful insights. With the 15th anniversary of 9/11 coming that September, I decided it was time to step out with my story.

As a social outlier, I have always seen things differently. This is something I struggled to understand about myself until 9/11 when I was jettisoned to a new, emotional place with the heartbreaking loss of my husband and the massive devastation of the attacks themselves.

In the fall of 2013, I started a company, a tactical and philosophical brand of kindness, and began teaching women to knit as a functional meditation. While it was great to connect with people one-by-one and share my vision, I was itching to spread the word on a larger basis.

Time was of the essence, and I decided that the best, most effective way to share my message would be with a public speaking platform. That summer a publicist friend wrote and distributed a press release based on the prompt: *Can we see 9/11 in a new light? Maybe it was a catalyst to open our world.*

Thirty-five radio and television stations, in small- to medium-sized markets from across the country, responded. My status and story as a 9/11 widow was newsworthy enough to garner some attention. From these interviews I became more confident that enough time had passed that people could hear a different story of 9/11. I also learned that, in order for my message to be considered credible in the world, I needed to write a book.

* * *

In the years that followed 9/11, two questions emerged: Why had we been so emotionally unprepared to handle 9/11? And where was all the wise counsel to help us through it? These questions became the foundation of my emotional, intellectual, and psychological analysis over the past seventeen years.

Seeking answers to these questions, I visualized a three-legged stool with a physical, an intellectual, and an emotional leg. Prior to 9/11 our American culture focused on the intellectual leg with the result being that many kids now achieved

4.0 grade point averages and perfect scores on their SATs. We focused on the physical fitness leg resulting in professional and Olympic athletes regularly setting new world records. But we had done nothing to develop the emotional leg. Because of this imbalance, when we were attacked on 9/11, our three-legged stool tipped over, and it seems we have been stuck there ever since. Now, seventeen years later, we can decide to make the effort to set that stool upright.

We haven't done anything wrong intentionally. We just haven't chosen to apply our resources to the emotional education of our children and ourselves. Seventeen years in the scheme of history is not much. But maybe enough time has passed that we can begin to look at our post-9/11 world from a more emotionally educated point of view.

Finding the positive light in this dark situation became my life's work. My view of life changed completely when I realized that struggles happen *for* us, not *to* us. We can actually choose to not be victims. All it takes is a shift in perspective.

Was 9/11 a birth canal to a new future? As chaotic and frightening as that might sound, great change always comes with great pain. Perhaps the extreme pain of 9/11 also means that the positive outcome and social correction can be equally extraordinary.

Life is not about just surviving. It is about thriving. "*Surthriving*." Life presents us with traumas and life presents us with tragedies. Living on the planet in the third dimension is about how we learn to handle these situations and better manage ourselves in the face of our challenges.

As human beings we have free will—we always have a choice: Do we want to live in fear and chaos, or do we want to live in our *personal power* and find positive solutions for a happier and more peaceful life? *Personal power* means finding our strength from within and learning to trust our inner knowing instead of looking outside ourselves for answers.

What if we learn from our experiences and become better for having lived them? We have a choice to shift from the fear-based paradigm that started when The Towers fell to a more positive mind-set. We can choose to see the light. But first we need to calm down and rationally consider the situation.

The Light in 9/11: Shocked by Kindness, Healed by Love is part of a thirty-year campaign to bring *Cozmeena Enlightened Living*, a brand of kindness, to the world. The vast and intricate story of how the *Cozmeena* concept came to be and where it is going will be presented in three books.

The Light in 9/11 is the first of the three. It is the microstory—my personal memoir of life and family and how the events surrounding 9/11 became the catalyst for my dramatic personal change. I hope that in hearing my story you will begin to trust me because I have so much more to share. Book Two will be the macrostory: the story of you and of our world together. Book Three will be about how we can create our beautiful future.

It is my sincerest wish to be able to help people to feel better, to see what they have instead of what they don't, and to live lives of joy and grace instead of fear and suffering.

● ● ●

One of the themes of my story is how the insidious effect of many "small" slights—accumulated over years and coming from many different relationships—can profoundly undermine the development of a child's self-esteem and self-confidence creating insecurity and self-doubt. Large traumas such as physical or sexual abuse are obvious, but it's the subtle, insidious, emotional *slights* that no one sees—but a child feels strongly—that can have devastating short- and long-term effects becoming deeply rooted in the child's psyche and emotional mind. They can cause self-hatred, depression, and personality disorders, and can build to a point of rage and violence. In their extreme, they can lie at the root of suicide.

Siblings, parents, extended family members, friends, classmates, neighbors, coaches, teachers, and any others that have access to the child's emotional self can make "subtle slights" through off-handed, thoughtless, poorly-timed remarks and/or negative expressions. To the child or person receiving these messages, they can feel like an emotional gut punch, adding another negative story to their painful internal dialogue of how they don't fit in—that they are unlovable, worthless losers.

It is in this context that my story begins. But first, 9/11.

INTRODUCTION

When things are badly broken, shattered into a million pieces, all we can see is the dark disconnection from what was once whole. But within the cracks, between the many pieces, there is always space. It is through these cracks that the light can shine through.

Things went dark across America and throughout the world as the magnitude and disbelief of the 9/11 attacks reverberated with a horrified global audience who watched together as the two majestic icons, the North and South Towers of the World Trade Center, crumbled to dust in a matter of minutes.

9/11 broke all the rules. No one knew what to do. We were caught so far off guard and so unprepared that we didn't even have a plan to have a plan.

Two images come to mind. The first is a chicken running around with its head cut off. Not a pretty sight, but this is how the world felt to me in the first days and weeks after 9/11 as our minds darted and jerked, spinning in terrified circles. The second image is of a stagecoach barreling down a mountain-side in an old spaghetti western, coming precariously close to the edge of a cliff as it rounded sharp curves at high speed and out of control because the driver had let go of the reins.

In the days and weeks that followed 9/11, I sensed the pressure of a powerful, emotional centrifugal force that had begun to spin as a new fear of terrorism settled in at a cellular level.

We each experienced 9/11 in our own unique way. I was acutely aware of being awash in this out-of-control, spinning energy, with no guidance, wisdom, or help in sight coming from anyone, anywhere. That is when my instincts took over, and I trusted what I knew deep down inside. I blindly followed it without knowing where I was headed or what the outcome would be. I chose to take a different path, a path that seemed to go in the opposite direction from everyone I knew.

Throughout my life, I struggled to fit in, which left me lonely, sad, and confused. But as everything in life happens for a reason, it turns out that not fitting in was the best possible preparation I could have asked for to help me handle what I was given.

Because all the rules were broken, the ways in which we might have fixed things before no longer worked. The macabre celebrity that came with being a 9/11 widow allowed me a strange freedom—an emancipation from having to follow the rules. Furthermore, having always seen things differently, I trusted myself for the first time and realized that, although we had just been shattered, a new place from which to start might come from this devastation.

Although my story may be one of the most extreme versions within the 9/11 experience, in losing my husband, that does not diminish what happened to you. 9/11 was a catastrophic, collective trauma that every American shared as well as our global neighbors.

9/11 rocked our sense of safety and security and shook the foundation of everything we trusted. It was the emotional equivalent of having every bone in our bodies broken simultaneously. In one fell swoop, everything we knew or thought we knew changed forever.

I had no idea then about the power of kindness, nor did I have any understanding of the kindness of strangers. I had expectations of how my family would help me if something ever happened, but no expectations of anyone else. To my astonishment, it was the kindness of friends and strangers that never let up and kept me buoyant as I healed, which has allowed me to be here with you today, telling my story.

In sharing my story, I hope to show how you can not only survive what life throws at you, but you can ultimately thrive in your healing by shifting your perspective to gain new and remarkable wisdom that comes from your experience.

Quite simply, it's all in how you look at it.

We each see life through a uniquely refracted lens based on our personal life experiences. Just as a fingerprint or dust particle on a piece of glass refracts light at different angles instead of allowing the light to pass through straight and clear, so do our life experiences create uniquely refracted lenses from which we filter information and navigate our lives.

I loved my husband Teddy Luckett with all my heart. I was devastated beyond words by his death. He was my soul mate, my best friend, and the love of my life but now he was gone, and there were four of us left standing. On top of the loss of Ted, I couldn't believe the situation our country was now in.

I was facing the ultimate challenge as a mother. I had to find a way for my children and me not only to survive but also to thrive as we navigated through the maelstrom ahead of us. My very young children had their whole lives ahead of them. From my life experiences, I understood that was too many years to waste on victimization and fear. I had no idea how I would do it—all I knew is that one day we would be okay and that we would bring Teddy right along with us into the future.

As the title of this book is *The Light in 9/11*, you might be asking yourself, how can there be a positive side of such a horrific event? Think of the ancient Chinese principle of Yin and Yang. This principle says that Yin is negative and dark, and Yang is positive and bright. It is the interaction and balance between the two that maintains the harmony of the universe and will influence everything within it.

This is the best way I can describe my experience of 9/11. I was given the Yin, and then the Yang. This was not intentional or something I tried to do. It just happened. As you will learn, my 9/11 experiences unfolded so uniquely that I came to believe that they were orchestrated by something far greater than myself.

I was just as shocked and horrified, heartbroken and terrified, scared and worried as everyone else by the attacks on 9/11 and the incredible chaos that followed. Above that, I had lost my life partner and the father of my children. Now I had our three babies, who would never know him, to protect and care for through this nightmare. How could Ted be gone? How could this be happening to us? I could not get my head around it. In a way, I still can't believe it's real, which actually works fine for me; somehow, it has never seemed final.

As the dust began to settle in the first few weeks that followed, my warrior instincts kicked in. From deep within me came a mission: I would not let Ted and all the others die in vain. I had to make something good come from this nightmare. I had to do something to make sense of it somehow.

Without knowing it then, I was setting a clear and powerful intention that would take my children and me on the most remarkable journey to discover an amazing and enlightened life that I could have imagined only in my wildest dreams. And Teddy has been in our hearts guiding us the entire way.

From shifting my lens to see the many facets of 9/11, studying them from every conceivable vantage point, I feel that I now understand how we can all shift our points of view without losing our *personal power*, and how we can respectfully coexist.

Which brings me to you. With commitment, patience, time, and conscious introspection, you, too, can realize incredible personal growth and wisdom. Most importantly, no matter how big or painful or life-changing an experience can be, there is no reason to give up hope or feel like you'll be lost in the darkness forever. Because given enough time, you can choose to see the light between the cracks and find the silver linings in your life's experiences.

CHAPTER ONE

9/11: THROUGH THE CRACKS
THE LIGHT WILL SHINE

SEPTEMBER 10, 2001

I wish I could tell you that everything was fabulous. That I was happily skipping through life smelling the roses, listening to the birds sing, and feeling grateful in the knowledge that I had three healthy children, a husband who loved me, and a nice roof over my head—but then, I'd be lying.

On the morning of Monday September 10, 2001, I was pissed. Ted had just called to ask if he could spend the following weekend—two full days—sailing in a regatta in Atlantic City. In my most loving, heartfelt response, I barked, "Are you effing kidding me? Absolutely not!"

I was drowning. And wound like a top. Postpartum depression had reared its ugly head, but I didn't know it then. Being thirty pounds overweight didn't help. I had learned I was six weeks pregnant in September 2000, and Timmy, my "fortieth birthday surprise," was now four months old. There I stood, in my size eighteen Talbots pants, with milk leaking through my shirt while the rose-colored glasses of motherhood dropped to the floor and were crunching beneath my feet.

I knew what I was in for with my third child—two years of being sidelined. No personal space or adult fun in my future. I was nursing Timmy as I had his sister and brother. To me, nursing a child meant being tied down and curbed. I missed my wine because I couldn't drink, but Ted could. Not good. My resentment, frustration, and anger brewed just below the surface. I loved my children, but at that moment, I wasn't so sure about my husband. I felt completely submerged, and there was no help in sight.

My daughter Jen was seven and had just started second grade. My son Billy was four and in preschool two hours a morning, four days a week. I did not have consistent babysitting help and I couldn't justify spending the money on a professional babysitter when I knew how fortunate I was to be home. So I jammed all my errands into those two hours that Billy and Jen were at school, as the thought of doing errands with three kids was too daunting even to consider. I was not a laid-back, easy-going mother; I needed to be efficient. I was edgy and inflexible. I could not seem to relax into it and find the rhythm that so many women seemed able to do. Being a mother of three was much harder than I had ever imagined. Inside, I felt unsatisfied, overwhelmed, and annoyed. But to the outside world, everything looked just dandy.

In 1997, I had been ready to stop working: I had satisfied all my goals in my fifteen-year sales career. I thought that being a stay-at-home-mom would be magical, fulfilling, and fun. Instead, now seven years into parenthood, I found it to be tedious, mind-numbing drudgery. I desperately missed using my mind and having meaningful adult interaction. Don't get me wrong: I loved my kids, and I loved Teddy Luckett. I knew I was fortunate, but nonetheless, on September 10, 2001, I was a miserable mess.

I had worked until Jennifer was two and a half when we left New York City to move to the New Jersey suburbs. I knew what it meant to be a working mother and how difficult it was to do both jobs well. The changing financial industry and Teddy's job didn't make things any easier on us. As I was intimately familiar with the workings of Wall Street, I sympathized with Ted regarding the stress and difficulties he faced every day.

In August of 2000, Ted had switched jobs within his company to a start-up: an electronic trading platform called ESpeed. The Internet, having debuted in 1993, was still relatively new, and the company's growing pains were plentiful. They struggled with how to structure the compensation, because there were no tangible transactions to account for. There was constant turnover in staffing. No one knew if they would have a job the next week.

Like so many working parents, Teddy felt the responsibility and pressure to provide for our young, expanding family, so his stress was extraordinary. He was up at 5:00 AM and not home again until 8:00 PM on the nights when he wasn't required to be out entertaining. He barely saw the kids. He was frustrated by this and tired of playing the game. I did my best to be supportive but found myself ruminating with resentment and frustration each night when he took the kids upstairs to have a bath and I was left to clean the kitchen. The housework was endless. The work of life was endless. I understand this is typical for all young parents, but that fall, I was in an especially bad place.

Still, I thought I was capable of handling everything. Like so many women, I had been conditioned in my upbringing to never ask for help. I needed Ted to take on more responsibility at home and be more hands-on with the kids. I needed him to *see* what it was I needed—I didn't want to have to ask him. I'm sure he, too, needed more from me than I was giving. We were both off-kilter and caught up in our own worlds. Sometimes, he would say that as much as he loved the kids, he couldn't wait until it was just the two of us again. Even though we were soul mates, I see now that Ted and I were in two very separate and unhappy places.

He got home that Monday night around 8:00 PM, and we finally got the kids to bed around 10:00 PM. It was then that we had the biggest fight of our marriage. Combing my wet hair and barking with each angry stroke, I snarled, "How could you be so inconsiderate to even *ask* me if you could go sailing? Can't you see that I'm drowning? The weekends are our only time with you and the only time I have help with the kids. I've been so angry all day that we might as well get divorced." Yes, I actually said this. I continued, "If I'm going to spend more days like this, let's just cut our losses now."

To this he replied, "Well, I thought I was being considerate to even ask you."

I guess that, based on my level of aggression, that was a fair response—but it made me even angrier and so I raged on. Still, he listened patiently in that quiet way he had that always calmed me down. When I finished my rant, he said,

"Well, I'm sorry to hear you had a bad day, babe. They fired ten more people today, so TJ and I are the only ones left."

That stopped me in my tracks, and everything snapped back into perspective. Having been heard, my anger was diffused and my frustration vented. Now that I understood what he was going through, I felt badly about how I had behaved. I calmed down and apologized, and things were better. We sat quietly for a while, and that loving feeling came back. We slept nestled in our customary spoon that night, with his foot hooked around my ankle.

In the morning, as he was leaving to go to work, I whispered, "You are my soul mate, honey. I love you." He smiled over his shoulder and echoed the same. Then he walked out the door, and was gone.

SEPTEMBER 11, 2001 9:05 AM
I drove Jennifer to school a little late that morning because she hadn't been feeling well the day before. She had just started second grade in our comfortable little suburban town on the North Jersey Coast. The phone was ringing as I walked back into the house after dropping her off.

When I answered, a friend said to me, "Lisa, which tower is Ted in?!"

"The one with the antennae on it—why?" I replied.

I remember her next words exactly: "Well, turn on the television, because a plane just hit it and took off the top fifteen floors."

She didn't bother to ask me what floor he was on. In the seconds that it took for me to run to the television and turn it on, in my mind's eye I saw Ted dead on the ground. His office was on the 105th floor, two stories from the top.

I stood in front of the television with four-month-old Timmy on my shoulder and my four-year-old Billy's hand in mine. Together, we saw the horrific and intense scene: the gaping hole, the raging fire, and the black, billowing smoke engulfing the upper floors of the North Tower. But the building was still intact—I had a moment of hope—Ted wasn't dead on the ground, as I had imagined. It was then I saw the second plane hit the South Tower, and I knew we were in trouble.

I remember screaming, *"No!!! Ted!!! Ted!!! Ted!!!"* Billy says I was stomping my feet, but I don't remember that. Over and over my mind raced: *This is not happening. This is not happening. I'm having a nightmare. Please don't let this be true! Oh, my God!! Oh, my God!!! Oh, my God!!!! Ted!!!!!*

The next thing I knew, we were sitting on the couch. Billy was on my lap, and I was holding Timmy. I hadn't let go of either of them. Time stood still, and I felt a strange numbness set in. I began to move, knowing that I had to function. I know now that I was in shock and my fight reflex had kicked in: I had to protect my family. I was the mother of three very young children, and they were my first concern. Instantly, I began to listen to my instincts; for instance, I knew Jen should remain at school because she was safe there. I experienced an innate confidence in my own judgment. Nature, God, the Universe—something was directing me, showing me the way. From a deep internal knowing, I knew, in that moment, to take charge and trust myself.

The antenna for the PBS television station we watched for children's programming was on top of the North tower, the one that had been hit first, and within minutes of the second plane hitting the South Tower, the station dramatically went dark. 9/11 was in full swing. I changed the channel and found the same image on every network.

I called my parents in Maryland and told them what was happening. They packed quickly and headed up. Now it was 9:30 AM or so, and people were already coming to my house.

The phone started ringing. I answered every call. Teddy? No. Everyone was scrambling trying to account for family members and friends who worked in and around the World Trade Center. Lower Manhattan was in chaos.

Within an hour, all of the cell phones crashed.

As I watched the buildings burning my mind raced: *Come on, Ted! Come on, Ted!* I prayed that the firefighters could get to them, but, in my logical mind, I knew that climbing one hundred floors was an enormous and slow uphill battle. Time was critical. This fire was raging. But there could be heroes in these situations, right? They would be okay. They would make it out.

Ted and his friends had been in the first terrorist attack on the World Trade Center in February of 1993. After that experience, they talked about an exit strategy if it ever happened again. The guys said that the next time they'd go to the roof instead of walking down 105 floors. They had "joked" about keeping gas masks and parachutes in their desks. Now in my desperate mind, I wondered, *Had any of them really done that? Could that fantasy possibly be true?* After my initial relief at seeing that the top fifteen floors were not already on the ground, I desperately hoped for the chance that they were still alive. In my conscious mind, I knew it would be hours or even days before we knew anything for certain. It never dawned on me that the buildings might collapse.

As I watched that thick, black smoke pour out from underneath Ted's floor, my logical mind conflicted with my needing, wishing, terrified heart. Because of my experience with the first bombing in 1993, in the back of my mind I knew that anyone above the fire was probably already dead.

In that bombing, there had been no visible smoke outside the buildings; yet when Ted got home that night and took a shower, the water ran black for five minutes because he was covered in so much soot. The explosion in 1993 was a car bomb in the lower level of the parking garage below the North Tower. This time, it was clearly very different.

I wanted to believe in a magical outcome. Looking out toward the hours ahead, I held onto shaky hope, but I knew deep down that, in all likelihood, Ted would not survive.

Any house that you called in those early hours, the wife would answer. We all picked up, hoping it would be our husband on the other end. We began calling each other every fifteen minutes or so for any news; I answered each of these calls on the first ring. I was communicating with the other wives I knew from Ted's company, Cantor Fitzgerald, who lived across the Tri-State area.

I called one of my closest friends, whose husband worked at a company in the South Tower, which lost 175 people, and learned he and our three other friends who worked there were all, miraculously, out of the office that morning.

As the morning progressed, more and more people were accounted for. I heard through the grapevine that some Cantor wives had spoken to their men before they died. I never heard from Ted. None of the other wives from the ESpeed group ever heard from their husbands, either. They had gone in that morning for an early sales meeting. The ESpeed offices were in the southwest corner of the building, and I believe the plane came up from underneath them.

SEPTEMBER 11, 2001 9:59–10:28 AM

Forty-five minutes or so had passed since the second plane had hit the South Tower. Now twenty-plus people were in my house, and more were coming. No one knew what to do. People were wandering from room to room, milling around in shock. Stunned. Spinning. Wringing their hands. Watching the news that played on every channel.

I realized it was time to nurse Timmy. I went upstairs and walked into a serene, unexpected silence. Because I needed to respond to my child, Nature was taking care of me by forcing me to leave the chaotic scene. Thank you, God.

I tucked into my familiar chair with my beautiful baby boy and allowed myself to take the moment I was being given. But within a few short minutes, a friend walked into my room. His face was ashen.

With stunned hesitation, he said quietly, "Lisa, Ted's building just collapsed."

My stomach lurched—it hurts now as I write this—and my heart stopped.

We turned on the bedroom television only to see that it was the South Tower that had fallen, not the North. I thought, *Oh my God!! This is insane!! How can this even be happening???!!!*

But it wasn't Ted's building. With twisted relief, I thought, *he's still okay.*

The next thing I knew, a stream of my closest girlfriends flooded into my bedroom. They sat with Timmy and me, jammed together on the foot of my bed, squeezing into every possible space. Together we watched in disbelief as the remains of the South Tower slowly settled down in an enormous plume of billowing, gray dust.

The television newscasters were speechless. They, too, were lost in their own experience of what we were witnessing together, in real time. We sat there glued to the television with morbid preoccupation. We could not have looked away if we'd tried. My mind raced, *How is this possible? How could a building of that magnitude just collapse like that? Please don't let this be real. God, I thought the fire was bad, but now ... Oh, my God!! Where are we? What is happening? Holy shit! Holy shit!! Holy shit!!! Ted!!!!*

Time felt like it was standing still, but the minutes ticked by. And then, without warning, in Technicolor horror, like a Hollywood movie, the North Tower gave way, collapsing silently, in abstract and eerie slow motion.

I whispered out loud, "Goodbye, Teddy. I love you," in a room filled with deafening silence.

And my Teddy was really gone.

There was no doubt now.

The friend next to me let out a heartbroken gasp, the sound of which I have never heard before or since. She wrapped her arms around me, dropped her head on my shoulder, and sobbed. My heart clutched in agony. My stomach lurched and ached with shock. My mind went numb with disbelief. We were frozen. No one moved. I don't know how long we sat there together in shocked, stunned silence.

● ● ●

Still reeling from what had just happened, my friends and I made our way downstairs sometime before 11:00 AM. I remember nothing of those moments. Timmy was with me, having just been nursed, so maybe I changed his diaper and went through the comforting motions of motherhood on autopilot. But time had stopped in suspended disbelief.

My composure returned as I reentered the downstairs world. The emotional shock was reverberating. People were spinning. News was coming fast. The event was still unfolding in real time. All air traffic had been grounded. We watched the television slack-jawed and dumbfounded. Our shock prevented an early flood of tears, although they would come later. People were just too stunned. But you could feel the fear. The pervasive, dark energy of terror descended on us like a heavy pall, even though it was one of the most beautiful days of the year.

I could hear my front door open and close as my house continued to fill with people. The phone rang constantly. I never put it down. Even though I knew the situation was dire, I still clung to hope. Each time it rang, I answered, "Teddy?" No. Again? No. For every call that wasn't him, my heart sank further, knowing that we were that much farther from a miraculous outcome. As people came in, they shared what they had heard. Beyond that, we had only what people around the world were seeing along with us, simultaneously, on television—an unprecedented, dark moment that would change the world forever.

* * *

I watched myself move quietly through the chaos, consciously aware of how surreal it was. I felt weightless. I could see the dust particles dancing in the sunlight that streamed through the dining-room window. Somehow I was detached from and watching—more as a witness—to what was happening around me.

As the first hours passed, people continued to come in and out, touching base and taking stock of the situation. Two guys I had known from high school came by and were incredibly gracious in their concern and care. People like them shuttled news and information between the "base camps," the homes of the people who were still unaccounted for, as we all tried to find our footing in this insane experience.

Everyone was so worried about Teddy. He was so well loved. No one could believe something like this was even possible in our world. They wanted to be here for the kids and me, but I also understood that they needed to be here for themselves.

By late morning, we learned that Flight 77 had crashed into the Pentagon at 9:37 AM and that Flight 93 had crashed in Shanksville, Pennsylvania, at 10:03 AM. I remember hearing the stories of these two crashes over the first couple of weeks, but not much about them after that.

They must have gotten lost in the sensational drama of the South Tower and the North Tower collapsing, on live television, as everyone around the world watched it together. The World Trade Center dominated the 9/11 stories. My heart has always been with the families of the other two crash sites. I hope they got as much love as we did.

The fearful, pain-filled energy was almost tangible throughout my house. The horror of the situation, and this new experience of terrorism, stopped us cold. No one knew what to do, and in reality, there was nothing anyone could do. We were just immersed in it. As successful, high-functioning people, finding ourselves in any situation that was completely out of our control was very uncomfortable, and because our world had just shifted on its axis, we were in brand-new territory.

By late morning, in my heightened state of clarity, I continued to watch what was happening from a place afar. Every moment or two, the voice in my head said, *Can this be real? Can Ted really be dead? Is this actually happening?* Nothing would sink in. It was then in my strangely functional, bizarrely detached state of mind, that an incredible calm came over me. Maybe it was because everyone else was reacting, so I didn't have to. Maybe it was because I was in shock. But regardless of why, my mind focused clearly on three thoughts.

The first: that it could be so much worse. It could be twelve thirty in the afternoon, like it was in the first attack in February of 1993, and those buildings could be full (capacity was 50,000). As bad as this was, it could be exponentially worse, and we could be watching the deaths of thousands more people.

Second: that it would be two years. Two years to a "new normal," a term I had never heard before in my life. I knew to put my head down and go, to take things as they presented themselves. I knew not to look ahead or look back. I had be steady and focused and stay in the moment. Because things got very simple: it was about my three children. I had to get them through this; they were all that mattered.

And third: that life as we knew it was now changed forever. Everything in our world had shifted completely.

In that moment, I saw the big picture. Our country had just taken an irreparable blow. We were broken beyond comprehension. I couldn't process the reality of Teddy's death, the deaths of all the others, nor the destruction we had just witnessed. But I could see clearly that our world would never be the same. Maybe my shocked mind stayed in this bigger place because the harsh reality of what had just happened to Teddy, and therefore to my children and me, was just too horrible to fathom. But this ten-thousand-foot view stayed with me.

The television news reported pockets of people being found in the wreckage. One group walked up and out of the rubble on a staircase that was somehow left intact. Newscasters told stories of the firefighters, police officers, and Port Authority officers who had gone in to rescue people and had been caught in the collapse. It looked like hundreds of first responders had perished. The selfless efforts of those brave souls are the greatest example of the courage and strength of the human spirit and the kindness of strangers in action. They are the true heroes in this war they had never planned on fighting.

We received word that Ted's company, Cantor Fitzgerald, had set up a command center at the Pierre Hotel in New York and were encouraged to call for information or go there ourselves. Cantor's offices had been on the 104th and 105th floors of the North Tower.

We listened as television newscasters made up details based on assumptions and conjecture. In the first few days, the banner headlines that ran along the bottom of the television screens said five thousand to six thousand people had been killed. Cantor and the other companies scrambled to account for their people, but with their offices now gone, it was painstaking and slow.

The reported numbers of injured and dead changed constantly. The final number of those killed was half of the original estimates. We knew, however, that Cantor Fitzgerald had been hit hard, and it would be confirmed in the coming days that 658 out of the 960 employees had been killed, twice the number of casualties of any other company in either tower.

In the weeks that followed, emotional dimensions of the damage continued to unfold. I felt this constant rumbling of fear and uncertainty in my belly that was almost painful. I observed the people around me, and I watched the news. It seemed like everyone felt the same way: an undercurrent of fear had lodged itself at our core.

We could no longer relax. Every muscle was tense. We felt a new constriction in our chests. In our minds, we created doubt about things that had once been stable and normal. We tiptoed around anticipating that a new terror was waiting around every corner. Life became very serious. We stopped laughing. We were no longer naïve and carefree. Our imaginations were taking over where reality stopped, and we were becoming our own worst enemies.

In one sensational, unprecedented moment, the terrorists had achieved their goal. Our emotional foothold was rocked to the core as individuals and as a nation. It didn't matter if you knew a victim or what state you were living in—you no longer felt safe anywhere in America. Our foundational sense of security had been completely shattered.

I jumped to the reactionary conclusion that the attacks on 9/11 were the first of many future events in this new paradigm of living with terrorism in America. And while I didn't really know what that meant, I did know it was the first day of the rest of our lives living in this disturbing, new reality.

THE FIRST HINT OF LIGHT

An hour or two after the buildings had fallen, I distinctly remember standing in my dining room, looking around at all my friends and neighbors who were desperate in their fear and their pain. All I wanted to do was to help them, but I also knew there was nothing anyone could do.

It was then that I had the sensation of someone propping me up from behind. I remember thinking, *Whoa! Really?? Am I imagining this? Am I wishing for this? Teddy, is that you?* Looking back, I know now that a Higher Power was guiding me almost immediately.

People around me kept asking me what they could do for me, how they could help me, and what it was I needed. I could see how much they needed to help me. I understood this because I would have felt the same way. In a crisis, most of us feel a profound need to help. It is an instinctive, intuitive drive. I know now that we are really trying to soothe ourselves by helping others. With the shock and trauma of 9/11, this natural need to help was multiplied one-hundred fold. But in truth, there was absolutely nothing anyone could do for himself or herself or me.

I am naturally empathic. I could feel my friends and how deeply they were hurting. I could sense how frightened they were. Even though they saw me experiencing the worst possible scenario in losing Teddy, I was also with them in the bigger picture—the event itself. With all my heart, I desperately wanted and needed to help them, too.

I am a highly organized Virgo with an Alpha personality, a healthy dose of perfectionism, and a controlling nature. In a crisis, it's me who will take care of you. In addition, I was raised in the late '60s through the '80s during the Feminist Movement, when the message to women was that not only could we do it all, but also that to ask for help was a shameful sign of weakness and failure.

So, in my mind at that time, I didn't need help. I didn't want help. I could take care of everything. I always did. I was a superwoman, just as I'd been raised. I was fine. I was. Really. Everyone else needed more help than I did. I was okay. Seriously, I was okay. Or so I thought. I really was more worried about them.

I see now that I was blown wide open by the shock of Ted's death and the magnitude of the event of 9/11. It was then, in that moment of surreal, heightened awareness that an intuitive knowing set in. I had never felt anything like it. A voice of certain truth inside my head said, *Lisa, let them help you.*

In what would be the most important moment of my life, I got it. I "knew" it was right. In that instant, I clearly understood that, in order to help my friends and neighbors, who were so desperate in their fear and their pain, I would have to let them to help me.

My logical, egotistical mind screamed, *"Oh, no! Absolutely not!"*

But the pull of something greater was so strong and so solid that I had to follow it. It was coming from my heart, not my head. So I trusted it and let go of my coveted control.

In that moment of surrender, I passed through a metaphorical door and was immediately overwhelmed with waves of humility, gratitude, and grace—and the most remarkable feeling of love that has been with me ever since.

This was my first experience of a profound intuitive knowing, an intuitive guidance that became my trusted light. I would faithfully follow that guiding light through the weeks, months, and years after 9/11.

So I let people in. I allowed myself to receive. I opened my arms, and I opened my doors. I allowed their care. I allowed their kindness. I allowed their generosity. I allowed their love. I allowed people to soothe themselves by being with us in any way they needed. I allowed them to touch us, to be with us, and to bring us gifts and food. Was it uncomfortable? Yes. But every cell in my body told me it was the right thing to do, so I relaxed into it and allowed it. It was remarkable. It still is.

It was then that I began to see the positive all around me. I couldn't help but see the beauty in everything. I saw pure, unconditional love radiating from everyone. People were open and kind. They were genuinely caring for each other and me. They were welcoming and tuned-in with a new, graceful tolerance. While they may not have felt it inside, what I saw was stoic resilience and incredible poise. We were standing together, bonded in this horribly negative, catastrophic experience, and I was witnessing the best of the human spirit. While we were being brought to our knees in pain and fear and grief, I saw our collective courage and strength of character. I couldn't stop seeing the power and grace of our humanity. I saw unconditional love and functional willingness. I saw that we had each other and that we would get through this. I saw the light in 9/11.

. . .

Looking back, in the strangest way, I was actually prepared to handle Ted's death. This also explains why I found myself in this unexpected, calm, offensive position just hours after the attacks.

First of all, I had faced the very true reality of Ted's death in the first terrorist bombing of the World Trade Center in 1993, and secondly, throughout our eleven-year marriage, Ted's mother worried out loud and often that he was going to die of a heart attack.

THE WTC 1993 BOMBING

The terrorist bombing of the World Trade Center in 1993 was my first experience with terrorism. Ted and I had been married for a little over two years, and he had been working for Cantor Fitzgerald for about one year. I worked at a contemporary jazz radio station on the twentieth floor of the *Daily News* Building in midtown Manhattan. When I looked south from our offices, I could see clearly the unobstructed majesty of the two World Trade Center towers in the distance.

It was a sunny winter day on February 26, 1993, and I was monitoring competitive radio stations for advertising leads when I heard the news of the attack just minutes after it happened. I went straight to our newsroom to find out more. Believe it or not, we did not have a television at the radio station then, so I would not see any visual news coverage until I got home later that night.

As I looked to the south out the newsroom window, the sun was reflecting brightly off the towers, and things looked fine. There was no visible smoke, so I thought (in my naïve, magical ignorance), "He's fine. He must be okay."

The news director misinformed me that the explosion had been in a lower level of the public parking garage under the Vista Hotel, two buildings away from Ted's. This man seemed confident that the explosion wasn't too serious. How he knew this, I'll never know, but I think his calm, if not naïve, demeanor allowed me to fool myself about Ted's precarious situation.

Ted's mother called me shortly thereafter. She was in a panic because she was watching the television footage of people covered in soot, streaming out of both Towers, with first responders and emergency equipment parked outside the buildings. As they say, a picture is worth a thousand words, so, in my misguided negation, I calmly told her what I knew. I said that I had a reliable news source at the station, and that it didn't look like the explosion was life threatening. I tried to quiet her with reason and logic. I told her that I was sure Ted was fine.

I followed the story on the radio. Logically, they were evacuating the buildings, so I was not surprised that Ted didn't answer his phone when I called. Very few people had cell phones then. Had I been watching the news, like Ted's mother, I would have had a much different experience, but instead I was happily floating in my magical bubble of denial.

When I got home after work, I turned on the news and saw the television coverage from the day; it was so much worse than I had imagined. But somehow I was still confident that Ted was okay. While it was running on every station, I could also see that it was a continuous loop of the same footage. Even though it was a very serious situation that took the lives of six people who had been in the parking garage at the time, and injured one thousand others who were below ground in the PATH train station, it was soon contained and under control. In the back of my mind, all I could think was that the news media were hyping the story, scaring people further, and making it even worse than it was.

Ted called me from a bar sometime around 6:00 PM. It had taken him four-and-a-half hours to walk down and out of the building. He was with several other guys, who had walked down the 105 floors with him, and they were having a few very stiff drinks. He said he'd lost count at five or six but that he didn't feel the effects at all.

He finally got home around 7:00 PM and seemed tired but okay, despite his face and clothes being black with soot. I cried with relief when I saw him. I had been calmly negating the situation all day, but the reality hit me when I saw him standing there, exhausted and dirty, with the acrid smell of smoke filling our apartment.

Ted told me everything as he took a shower to wash off the soot and I numbly watched the black water go down the drain. He and the others had walked down in single file, holding the shoulder of the person in front of them. He said there were times when they would only take one step every twenty to thirty seconds and sometimes they had to get down on their knees and crawl across a huge landing to get to a different stairwell. He said the smoke in the stairwell became thicker the lower down they went. By the 80th floor, the lights went out, and they were in total darkness the rest of the way down.

As he relaxed, Ted told me that people had stayed relatively calm, and some were even cracking jokes. He said he felt fortunate to be with New Yorkers, because they were so tough-minded and didn't panic. Because he had gone in dressed casually that day, he was able to breathe through his sweater, but he still had a cough for several months afterward. When he got out of the building, all of Lower Manhattan was closed, so he had walked North to find a phone and a cab.

He said New York had never smelled so good. He was tired but relieved, happy to have finally made it out safely. He was in good spirits and seemed fine, just as I knew he would be. Ted's light-hearted nature made everything easy. That night I asked myself, *Why had I been so sure he was okay? Was I a crazy denier, or was it because I had known since we first started dating that we were connected as soul mates?*

The bombing was on a Friday, and we went out to Westchester County, New York, to see his mother the next day. On Monday, Ted and his desk mates were told they would be flying to London in two days, for an unspecified amount of time, to do business from the Cantor office there. This was very bad news. My big bubble of denial had popped over the weekend when I finally realized how incredibly dangerous the ordeal had been for him. We were both feeling a dark resonance from the experience, and now he was leaving. I was sick about it.

Like anything dreaded, though, the reality was easier than the expectation and Ted and his desk mates were back within two months. I went over for my first trip to London in the middle, which was actually quite magical. Oh, the idealism of youth.

The World Trade Center reopened the doors of both Towers a month after the explosion, but Cantor took extra precaution to be sure all the engineering specs and tests were well documented before moving everyone back into the offices on the top two floors of the North Tower.

Ted and the guys joked that they would keep gas masks and parachutes in their desks. But in all seriousness, they said the next time it happened, they would go to the roof. *The next time it happened?* Ugh! Why didn't they listen to themselves?

A HEART ATTACK

The other reason I was prepared for Ted's death was that his mother talked often about her worry that he was going to have a heart attack. I heard this almost every time I saw her for years.

Like many guys his age, at forty years old, Ted was a walking heart attack. He was managing the pressure and responsibility of taking care of our young, expanded family. He commuted long hours to a high-stress Wall Street job. He was thirty pounds overweight because he couldn't exercise or eat right on the trading desk. Like his mother, Ted also had naturally occurring high cholesterol, which did put him at higher risk for a heart attack.

Ted's father had died from cancer when Ted and his siblings were teenagers, and the family still grieved the loss. Because Ted's mom had experienced the trauma of losing her husband early, she was worried about Ted's health for the kids and me. I understood where she was coming from; with his statistics, she had reason to worry. She talked to him about it often, encouraging him to exercise and watch his diet, but like most of us with our worrying parents, he disregarded her pleas.

While her worry for him was genuine, for me it was slow, quiet torture. Hearing this constant prompting caused me to run his death through my mind literally hundreds of times. I would lie awake at night and run the scenario through my mind, getting myself very upset, often weeping with worry.

But eventually, when I couldn't torment myself any longer, we bought as much life insurance as we could afford and updated our will. I knew where all the important documents were kept and made sure that we went to bed peacefully at night, having righted any wrongs from the day. Then I tried to let it go.

The human imagination is very powerful. I can attest that not only can you get yourself just as worked up over the idea of an event, but also you can actually make it worse.

So on the morning of 9/11, because I had been mentally prepared by these two bizarre things, my shock was manageable, and I shifted to a place of calm, rational thinking. By late morning, I was "okay." In the strangest way, I was clear. I was capable. I was calm. I was also a nursing mother of a four-month-old, and Nature supported me so I would not go down.

As they say, the best defense is a good offense. I had spent so much time thinking about Ted's death that, when it actually happened, I found myself in a centered, offensive position, calmly able to handle things instead of being off-balance in a defensive position, reactive and emotional—where most people are regarding sudden death. So by early afternoon on 9/11, I was firmly grounded and able to manage what was coming at me. I was like a Weeble; I wobbled, but I didn't fall down.

Yes, I was devastated by Ted's death. Yes, I was very worried for my children. Yes, I was heartbroken at their loss, my loss, and the country's loss. Yes, I could see and feel that fear was seeping into our psyches like nothing we'd felt before. Yes, I was in disbelief that both Towers had actually fallen. Yes, I was worried for our national safety. Yes, I was in shock. Yes, I was reeling. But by being prepared in this twisted way, I was calm and rational and able to handle it.

. . .

9/11 blew me out of the proverbial box, a box created by my family and society that I had unsuccessfully tried to fit into for my first forty-one years. Suddenly I was free, emancipated, and liberated from those restrictive ties—somehow I knew that I no longer needed to adhere to the traditional thinking, beliefs, and habits of our pre-9/11 society.

As those first days passed, as much as my heart hurt and as worried as I was, a new sense of strength began to build inside me. Pain and fear became my fuel for action. I felt a power, a determination unlike anything I had ever known before.

I had become a warrior—not an angry, vengeful warrior—but a warrior of love. I felt a fierce love and a profound, positive strength. I stood in a solid place. I was a mother who would protect and care for her children. I would navigate my broken little family through this maelstrom. We would be okay. Every cell of my being told me my intuition was right. I began to trust myself instead of looking to others for answers.

In those early weeks, I vowed that I would never let Ted and all the others die in vain. I would spend my life making something good come from this nightmare. If I didn't, then the terrorists would win, and I could not let that happen.

Our psyches and our country had taken an unprecedented blow, but life would go on. We would come back, and if I had anything to say about it, stronger and better for having lived it. Without realizing it, I was setting the single greatest intention of my life.

My only weapon in fighting back was to figure it all out—and fast. I needed to dig in and find alternative solutions as quickly as possible. I sensed this clearly from a place deep within. I would take my kids forward, toward a positive future, and we would bring Teddy with us. With each step I took in this new direction, the path unfolded before me as something greater pulled me along.

To figure things out meant that I would need help. I was being given the opportunity to study the "why" of everything, and I was up for the challenge. After a lifetime of frustration, being misunderstood and misunderstanding, I didn't care what people thought anymore. I was caught in the middle of a world-changing catastrophe the likes of which had not been experienced in our lives. My mission was set. I had important things to figure out for my children, the world, and myself.

It was a time of being incredibly open. Shock and pain will do that. Nature took care of me. It gave me a necessary numbness. I went through my days in the current of life caring for my little kids. When I slept, I was blank. Although there was always a low hum of darkness and a great sense of worry that my children's and my futures were precarious, I was not often overwhelmed by it. Ted was always on my mind and I missed him terribly, but somehow I was soothed because I knew he was still with us. My children filled me with their joyful innocence and kept me in the moment. Baby Timmy saved me. When I was sad, all I had to do was look at his beautiful, happy face, and I would smile through my tears.

Events that occurred in the months that followed continued to affirm my belief that Teddy was still with us.

By the time Jennifer was in kindergarten, she and I didn't like each other. Although I felt enormous love for her we clashed often in a war of wills. She was naturally closer to

Teddy and they shared a deep and special connection. Rather than always fight an uphill battle, by the time Jen was in elementary school, I had become conditioned to pushing her off to Ted when things became difficult.

One day after losing Ted, Jen and I were standing in her room going toe-to-toe about something and my anger was escalating. I stopped myself then and said sincerely, "You know, Jen, if your dad was here, I would push you off to him. But he isn't here anymore so we are going to have to figure this out for ourselves."

In that split-second Jen changed right in front of me; I could almost see the light of realization click on in her mind. From that moment of awakening, she shifted to become the most loving, kind, considerate, and helpful daughter I could have ever asked for. She has never waivered nor slipped back into her old behavior since that day, nor have I.

Jen, too, must have become more open from the pain of her father's death. I have always felt that Ted was there helping us to forge this beautiful, loving mother-daughter bond that had been so painfully missing from our lives.

Another morning, I was taking Billy to his gymnastics class while Timmy stayed at home with a babysitter. It was unusual for the two of us to be alone in the car together and we were both enjoying the quiet moment as we drove along the familiar road.

From the back seat Billy said to me, "Mommy, I had a dream about Daddy last night. We were at the movies together and it was all white. He was wearing a white suit and he smiled at me." I told him how happy I was for him and asked him how it made him feel. He said, "It made me feel good."

I knew then that Billy had had a "visit" from Ted. The details he described were clear and specific, more than in a typical dream, and he was left with the telltale sign of feeling happy instead of sad.

We often underestimate the wisdom of children and how much they are capable of knowing.

CHAPTER TWO

BEACONS OF HOPE

Ted Sent Me Three People

A little bit about Ted Luckett. . . .

Teddy, to those who knew him, was marvelous. If you read the bios of every man who died in the World Trade Center, they all sound very similar. Great guy, loved by all, great father, great friend, wonderful husband. I'm sure this is true about all of them. But, to me, Teddy Luckett was one in a million.

Yes, he had those characteristics, but what made him special was his personable, lighthearted charm and loving, playful spirit. Ted warmed any room he entered with an easy-going energy and effortlessly entertained with clever, comedic timing. He was incredibly kind and never met a stranger.

I met Ted in the fall of 1986, after the most difficult year and a half of my young adult life. I had moved to New York in the spring of 1985 to try my hand at radio advertising sales after a successful three-year radio sales career in Denver. And New York had kicked the shit out of me.

People often asked me why I left beautiful Denver when I had an established life, fun friends from college, a good career in the making, and a great cost of living. In those first eighteen months in New York, I asked myself the same thing many, many times.

In the summer of 1980, I had worked as an intern at *Yachting Magazine* and was immediately consumed by a driving need to one day live and work in Manhattan. I had to have the energy, the intensity, and the excitement of the Big Apple. I remember walking from the train at Penn Station to my office on Park Avenue wanting to *skip* for the sheer joy of being there. If I had a tam o'shanter hat like Mary Tyler Moore, I would have thrown it up in the air as I crossed the street.

I knew it was time to leave Denver when a friend came back telling yarns about his trip to New York. I felt this bratty sense that New York was mine. Many years later, I would feel the same proprietary ownership of Colorado when people spoke of going there. I think I have a condition—I don't share very well.

In those first eighteen months in New York, I struggled to find my footing in business (and life) but ultimately found success selling one of the oldest and best-known radio stations in the country, WOR-AM.

In October of 1986, Ted and I met through a mutual friend named Dan, and the three of us spent the first six weeks of our new friendship cavorting and playing as young, upwardly mobile professionals—Yuppies—in and around New York City.

It had been a painfully lonely time, and I was starved for human connection, having arrived in New York to find myself struggling, isolated, and alone. I was so desperate for friends that as cute as Teddy was, I didn't want to ruin my first real friendships in New York by dating him. So without realizing it, Ted and I were courting, and Dan was our chaperone.

That fall, the three of us spent much of our time meeting for lunch or after work for drinks. Our favorite mode of communication was quoting movies. Ted and I were especially good at this.

The first night Ted, Dan, and I hung out together was at PJ Clarke's on 53rd Street and Third Avenue, one of the oldest bars in New York. While drinking Martinis and Manhattans, Ted and I started quoting the classic 1981 movie *Arthur*, with Dudley Moore. It was then I knew I had met the man of my dreams. We ricocheted back and forth, line for line, without missing a beat, reciting our favorite quotes in random order:

> *"Oh, you're a hooker?! I thought I was doing great with you!"*
>
> *Arthur to his butler: "Remember when we used to play hide-and-seek, and you never found me?"*
>
> *Butler to Arthur: "Do you know I never looked?"*
>
> *Fiancée he doesn't want to marry to Arthur: "Arthur, take my hand."*
>
> *Arthur to his fiancée: "That would leave you with one."*
>
> *To the waiter bringing his scotch: "The doctor says I must have ten of these an hour."*
>
> I could go on for hours.

Years later, when Ted and I were married and living in New Jersey, Jen was four and Billy was one year old and I was struggling with being a full-time, at-home mom. It had been a particularly difficult day, and I was complaining to Ted about Jennifer's behavior.

After I ranted for five or ten minutes, while Ted listened patiently, he finally said, "So what you're telling me is she's a candidate for boarding school." I burst out laughing. As he did so many times during our lives together, Ted's kind and clever humor calmed me down and diffused my tension.

Anyone who knew Teddy Luckett would agree that he had the gift of finding levity in difficult situations, relieving the pressure without being (too) inappropriate, and that he shared his lighthearted love and kind, graceful spirit freely and generously.

. . .

By late October 2001, the shrill and chaotic intensity of what we'd been living through dissipated a bit and life took on a new rhythm. I was still so open to what I was experiencing that I watched as things presented themselves. Within six weeks of 9/11, Teddy sent me three people who showed me the possibilities of a new future.

MRS. DOUBTFIRE

By early November, I was in desperate need of help. My mother and brother had left, and I couldn't impose on friends to help me with the kids. People were busy with their own lives, and I needed to find some structure and routine. I needed a Mrs. Doubtfire.

I put an ad in a local paper that literally said, "Looking for Mrs. Doubtfire." A close friend recommended an older woman who lived in the next town over, saying, "I only wish Maureen could raise *my* kids." I hired her on the spot, and Maureen became our Mrs. Doubtfire.

Wise, pragmatic, and caring, Maureen had seen it all. Maureen had married Charlie, a family friend, who had been widowed shortly after Maureen's divorce, fifteen years earlier. Maureen had been a friend of Charlie's wife, and their children had played together in the neighborhood where they lived.

For Charlie's two daughters, Maureen was a connection to their mother. Maureen's children gained a kind and thoughtful stepfather. There were four children in their blended family: three girls and one boy. The children had been in elementary school when Maureen and Charlie married. When I met them, the kids were in their early twenties.

Maureen and Charlie scooped us up and brought us into their fold. Jen, Bill, and Tim would go there for sleepovers. I could drop Timmy off for the afternoon. Maureen and Charlie's young-adult children embraced my kids like little cousins. Although I paid Maureen, it was secondary to how we felt about her. Thinking back now, I should have paid her so much more. We didn't just get Maureen—we gained an entire family. Thank you, my dear Teddy.

Maureen would tell me to take time for myself. She saw that I was drowning. She encouraged me to get out and do things alone. She kept Timmy for me the first time I took Jen and Billy skiing that winter and when I took them to Williamsburg in the spring. I felt this intrepid need to travel with my children and prove that we would forge on, that we were unstoppable, that we would be okay.

Maureen never knew Ted; she knew only me. She saw in me a relatively young, widowed woman with a lot of time ahead of her. Having not known the person who died, she only saw the person who was living. She had no guilt or (perceived) disregard of Ted. To Maureen, it was simple: it was about me.

Not only did Maureen help me with my children, she showed me a future with possibilities. Maureen's stories of marrying a second time and raising a blended family gave me hope. It had not been easy, but they were a close family of very good people. They loved each other and pushed through the difficulties, despite the struggles of a complicated family life.

Maureen was in her late fifties when she came to us, and the wear-and-tear of managing a young family was too physically demanding. Sadly, she had to stop coming in on a daily basis after about eight months, but she was the priceless, loving bridge I needed to get me over the first hump. Maureen remained in my corner as my friend and wise counsel for many years.

A THERAPIST

I felt like 9/11 was the emotional equivalent of breaking every bone in my body simultaneously. Just as logical people would seek medical attention for their bodies, I went to the doctor for my mind.

I wanted to get Jennifer started in therapy as soon as possible. I would find a therapist for myself once she was settled. In my enlightened, out-of-the-box, intuitive state of mind, I knew this was critical to taking us through the quagmire we were facing. I didn't have the answers. My family and friends didn't have the answers. It was clear to me that the leadership of our country, from government to corporate America, had no idea what to do, and the religious organizations were scrambling.

I met Dr. VK, PhD Clinical Psychologist, in late October 2001. She was the third therapist on a list of practitioners referred to me for Jennifer. Having had a good experience with therapy in New York ten years before, I knew the patient-practitioner relationship was a unique one that required a special connection and I was determined to find this again.

While explaining my background, Dr. VK asked me why I didn't go back to my previous therapist in New York. I told her that I believed there were good people everywhere. Also, with three very small children, running into New York, even for a day, was difficult at best. She asked me why I was interviewing therapists. After a moment's thought, I replied, "Well, I've had a lot of bad dentistry"—meaning that not everyone who has a degree in something is good at what they do.

True to my belief that there are good people everywhere Dr. VK proceeded to blow my mind with her depth of knowledge, her extensive education, and her vast experience. In that first hour, she effectively rooted out my situation with excellent questions. I had found a world-class therapist, an expert in her craft, right in my little town just minutes from my house. I had found my match. I had gone there for Jennifer and left with an appointment for myself.

Jennifer started seeing a seasoned art therapist named Stephanie Hagadorn (may she rest in peace), who was warm and kind and very groovy. I would describe Stephanie as Mama Cass meets Granny Good-Witch. She was artistic and alternative, using a therapeutic technique called Sand Tray

Play. Dr. VK and I managed Jennifer's therapy with Stephanie, giving Jennifer the benefit of two seasoned therapists and one very loving mom.

Jennifer is an anomaly. Since the age of seven, she has received respectful consideration as the individual that she is. She has always been given the straight story while being fully supported by three intelligent, professional, and genuinely caring women. Because of this, I believe Jennifer Luckett is one of the most emotionally educated young women her age.

I don't go often, but I still see Dr. VK to this day. All these years later, outside of my children, she is the single most valuable relationship I have. Now I think of analysis as my favorite sport. Dr. VK and I have never crossed the line into friendship, although we experience great friend-like love. We have reached the place where we are so aligned in our respective understanding that we often cocreate in theory and insight regarding the future, both micro and macro.

In the early phase of writing this book, I told Dr. VK that I thought the book was going to be about psychotherapy. This was her response: "Your book is about far more. Therapy allowed you to develop the capacity to feel all your feelings without disruption in your goals, to understand your imaginings and fantasies and not act on them. This facilitated recorrective experiences where true separation from the past freed creativity, spirituality, and intelligence."

Dr. VK is an emotional resource for Jen, Billy, Timmy, and me that is a very rare find in this life. Thank you so much, My Sweet Teddy.

A BUSINESS PARTNER AND THE BEGINNING OF MY SPIRITUAL EDUCATION

In mid-October of 2001, our neighbors Bruce Springsteen and Jon Bon Jovi joined an already-scheduled concert at a local, historic theater. The concert had been planned before the attacks on September 11, 2001, and the musicians were groups from the 1970s produced by the Sun Records Company, best known for Elvis Presley, Carl Perkins, and Johnny Cash.

In the first days after 9/11, the producer of the concert, a man named Rick K, created the Alliance of Neighbors of Monmouth County charity concept on the sidelines of a Pop Warner football practice. He donated the concert's proceeds to be the first fundraiser for the Alliance of Neighbors. The charity's premise was to provide financial relief for the families in our county who had lost a loved one in the attacks.

The show was a spectacular success. Jon Bon Jovi opened with a fantastic, upbeat gospel song, with the local Baptist Church Choir singing back up, and Bruce Springsteen performed several songs and closed with an incredible finale. The night raised more than $1 million for The Alliance of Neighbors of Monmouth County Foundation.

Charitable foundations were popping up everywhere. Almost all of the 2,832 people who had died had some kind of fundraiser held in their honor or charity started in their memory. It seemed that raising money was the only thing people could do to salve the open wound left by 9/11. People's continued kindness would reach precedent-setting levels.

I had been invited, along with several other widows, to meet Bruce Springsteen at the dress rehearsal for the concert.

Because of this, Rick called me a few days after the concert to see if I would be willing to be interviewed on CNN's *Greta Van Susteren Show*. I agreed, and we were escorted by limousine into New York City the next night.

On the way to CNN, an inspired and personable Rick regaled me with stories from the time he spent with the late singer-songwriter, Carl Perkins and the psychic medium, John Edwards. Both men understood how our loved ones communicate with us from the Other Side.

Rick's background had been in music and television production. In the early 1990s, he had been the personal assistant to Carl Perkins, who wrote "Blue Suede Shoes" and inspired groups like the Beatles, U2, and Roy Orbison. Carl Perkins was a spiritually enlightened man.

Rick had also worked with John Edwards to help sell his television show, *Crossing Over*, to the Sci-Fi Channel in the late 1990s. During the time they had worked together, both Carl Perkins and John Edwards had shown Rick the vast and remarkable world of the Other Side; our spiritual connection to those who have crossed over and how they take part in our daily lives.

That night on the way to New York, Rick told me about signs. How they came in the form of music, numbers, and through electronics. He said to pay attention to things that repeatedly showed themselves, that there were no coincidences, and serendipitous events had meaning.

I had heard smatterings of this before, but never with such in-depth description by someone who had experienced them up close and personally. It was charming. I was enthralled and bolstered by this new perspective. Here was a positive way to cope with Ted's loss, and it resonated with me completely. As lost and alone as I had been feeling, this lighthearted, enlightened way to connect with Teddy felt right. It seemed like the natural progression of the intuitive enlightenment and sensory pull I had been experiencing since the morning of 9/11.

I brought this enlightened thinking home and taught my kids. Rick's knowledge confirmed an interest I'd had in the metaphysical for many years. The idea of the collective soul had always resonated with me: that we are eternal and never really die; our energy just changes form. The kids and I saw signs everywhere we looked. Teddy showed us his love in the sunsets at night and spoke to us through special songs on the radio. What is faith but believing in that which we cannot prove? It was our choice, and it worked for us. We began to live by this new, playful code, and we still live by it today. It is the foundational thinking of this book and the ones that will follow.

With the success of the Alliance of Neighbors Concert, Rick was excited to produce other shows in a continued effort to raise money for the foundation. He seemed genuinely inspired and motivated to help in this way. He had a concept called a docu-concert and wanted to combine the Alliance of Neighbors Concert footage with interviews of local widows, friends, and neighbors telling their personal stories of 9/11.

Even around something as sacred as 9/11, things often become political. Rick began to be upstaged and pushed out by the manipulations of people involved in the Alliance. I witnessed their bullying of him at a meeting one night. Bullying gets my attention. I sensed that Rick was receiving unfair treatment and had a strong, intuitive pull to help him.

I thought the docu-concert concept was inspired. I enjoyed Rick's positive, upbeat energy, which was a refreshing change from everything else around me. Having received so much from so many in such a short period of time, I was pleased to find someone whom I could help.

I was also intrigued by his unique business idea and the industry of event production. I was having such a strangely beautiful experience that I wanted to share it with others in some big way. Here was a chance to do something creative and positive amid the negativity of 9/11; it was a chance to swim against the tide of fear that was surrounding us.

Rick and I started a business partnership in early November of 2001. Working offered me a healthy and much-needed distraction. I was feeding my starving mind, I was gaining new knowledge of concert and television production, but, more importantly, I was learning the language and teachings of the Other Side and became immersed in the world of spiritual enlightenment. Again, I thank you, My Beautiful Teddy.

CHAPTER THREE

LOST IN THE DARKNESS OF MISUNDERSTANDING

Where I Came From, Where I Was

I am the product of what could commonly be called the typical American family. From the outside looking in, we appeared normal. We were physically healthy, lived in a nice house in a nice town, had nice clothes to wear and plenty of food to eat. We were very fortunate.

The members of my family—my grandparents, parents, and siblings—were good people and I know everyone did their best in the circumstances we were given. I understand that the damage I incurred growing up was completely unintentional. But just days before my birth, my young family was dealt a devastating hand by a series of tragic events that would negatively shift the trajectory of our family forever.

Society had not yet evolved to understand the emotional skills necessary to manage trauma nor were the nuances of a child's emotional sensitivity yet considered. The adults in my family did not have an understanding of how to handle the pain, anger, and grief that followed their sudden and excruciating trauma. As a result my life was a struggle from the start.

Behind the scenes of our idyllic setting, my family struggled with generational alcoholism and unresolved emotional issues. My ancestors and my parents had no educated form of emotional release and little healthy expression of their feelings.

As children, my brother and I lived with the trickle-down effect of this damage: emotional neglect, alcoholic anger, and enabling denial. This caused subtle, and not-so-subtle long-term damage that I carried well into adulthood.

• • •

As a result of 9/11, I experienced a "great correction."

To explain this positive shift, it is important to give you the details of how the consistent subtle slights that I received from all corners of my life became the foundation of my life story—how I saw myself, and how I fit into my family and the world.

All four of my grandparents were born in 1907 and were of the Interbellum Generation—they were too young to fight in World War I and too old to fight in World War II. From early childhood, they knew only a troubling and changing world. They were children during World War I and lived through Prohibition and the Roaring Twenties in their teens and early twenties. They entered young adulthood facing the poverty and scarcity of the Great Depression and the Dust Bowl; they experienced the fear and devastating darkness of World War II all before they were forty. My grandparents' lives were shaped and molded in the thirty-two years between 1914 and 1946.

My parents were born in 1934 and 1935, in the middle of the Great Depression. At age seven, my father remembered when the Japanese bombed Pearl Harbor in 1941. He spoke of the rationing and shortages that affected everyone in World War II. With the men off fighting the war, women joined the workforce for the first time, leaving home to work in the factories. Everyone did his or her part to help in the war effort. My mother told me how even as a child she and her friends separated the aluminum foil from gum wrappers to make into balls to donate to the cause.

Fear and emotional trauma were common in those years. However, even with all the shared pain, loss, and fear, the strict social edicts of the time dictated tight and closed emotional behavior. While every community suffered loss and emotional hardship from the deaths of sons and fathers killed in action, the sadness from their pain and grief was typically kept inside and, for the most part, left unspoken.

The only acceptable place to go for emotional support was their place of worship. Since the founding of the United States of America, organized religion is about the only form of stigma-free emotional education in our society.

From what I can tell from literature, movies, television, and family stories, normal behavior in American society from the 1900s through the 1950s was predominantly silent, terse, and formal with strict moral codes and restrictive, judgmental rules. Conversation regarding emotional needs was rare. I believe the repression and denial of the painful human emotions experienced during those turbulent years lies at the root of the social dysfunction we are experiencing today from our leadership centers down to the family unit.

• • •

Growing up, I heard how my parents' childhood experiences shaped their lives. As part of the Silent Generation, they went to high school and college in the 1950s. The postwar boom brought prosperity to America. After decades of struggle, a light shone in the darkness when World War II ended in 1945. The cultural landscape that emerged in the late 1940s and 1950s created societal norms and fashionable stereotypes of what the contemporary American Family was supposed to look like and how it was supposed to act. This was the model my family structure was built on.

MY FATHER'S FAMILY

From the outside looking in, my father's family would appear to have lived the perfect American Dream.

My father's grandfather, Carl Peterson, emigrated from Sweden in the early 1900s and achieved success as an inventor of motors and generators before World War I. His company, The Star Electric Motor Company was awarded U.S. Naval contracts beginning in 1914 that would continue through World War II. By the late 1930s, his company was very successful and employed more than 4,000 people.

My father's parents, Milton Lindeman and Margaret Peterson, had three children: Neil (my father) in 1934, Judy in 1938, and Marsha in 1948.

Margaret was ahead of her time having graduated from Business College in 1930. She became a trusted employee for the Star Electric Motor Company working in the accounting department.

Neil was the first-born son to his parents and the first-born grandson to his maternal Swedish grandparents, Carl and Merta Peterson. The Petersons would become the dominant family relationships in my father's life growing up.

My father's grandmother Merta was a dominant matriarch. My father told us about his grandmother's antagonism toward his mother. Margaret was successful in her life. After graduating from college she started a career and married a good man. Her younger sisters Ruby and Pearl, who it seems were favored by their mother, did not do as well despite being given the same advantages. Alcohol was a common denominator in the family and my great-grandmother and her three daughters were heavy drinkers. From my father's stories it sounded to me like the Petersons lived in a wealthy, privileged household with a lot of conflict and some very spoiled and unhappy people in it.

As the first-born grandchild in this wealthy immigrant family, my father had all the bells and whistles that went with his privileged position. Because his parents never properly reined in his intelligent and reactive personality and, while he could be charming, he was allowed to become a young tyrant: arrogant, aggressive, and dominant.

In the summer of 1950, my father's life changed abruptly when his father, Milton, died unexpectedly. It was a Sunday afternoon, and Milton and Margaret were crewing for my father in his 16-foot sloop while sailing on Barnegat Bay. My grandfather suffered a stroke and died before they reached the dock. Milton had been a young man with a young family and was loved by all who knew him. The loss rocked their small community.

After Milton's death, as was the norm for the times, Margaret made fourteen-year-old Neil the "man of the house." Although crushed by the loss of his father, he stoically accepted his new responsibilities and stepped up as the dominant male in the household. I suspect that he subconsciously took on the emotional responsibility for his father's sudden death, a burden that stayed with him throughout his lifetime.

But as man of the house, young, sensitive Neil repressed the grief and sadness of losing the father he loved. Since boys were never supposed to cry, the only outlet for my father's pain and grief was anger; this would become the channel he used to handle all uncomfortable, sad, or negative emotion throughout his lifetime.

When my father was fifteen–the summer after his father's death–and even though he was the "man of the house," his mother encouraged him to leave the East Coast to go work on his uncle's dude ranch in the Colorado Rocky Mountains because she knew how much he needed the change of scenery.

It seems that my father found solace and comfort caring for the horses and cattle amid the beauty of the Colorado High Country. I would watch his disposition change and he would become softer and deeply soulful when he told us stories about his favorite animals and the time he spent in the quiet mountain setting. I believe he felt love for this special time and place because without realizing it he processed his grief there.

He continued going to the ranch in the summers throughout high school and stayed West for college, attending Colorado

A&M (now Colorado State University) from 1953 to 1957, majoring in animal husbandry.

. . .

Within the ten years after Milton's death, my grandmother Margaret remarried and divorced twice, both times to men who were alcoholics. This brought extreme criticism upon Margaret by her mother Merta and sisters Ruby and Pearl because of the shame divorce brought to the family. In spite of this, Margaret generously took in Ruby and her three daughters when Ruby herself divorced in the mid-1950s. I do not know why Merta did not take in her own daughter and granddaughters, but my father said she continued to be an overbearing and unpleasant matriarch who meddled and interfered in their lives.

. . .

My parents were born within months of each other but they were from completely different worlds.

MY MOTHER'S FAMILY

My mother, Connie, was born in Topeka, Kansas, in 1935, the only child of Roy and Viola Keifer Trompeter. Both Roy and Viola came from the same small farming community in northeast Kansas, but they had different life experiences there. They attended the same one-room schoolhouse along with their brothers and sisters, where all grades were taught together.

From the stories I was told, Viola's family were poor tenant farmers, while Roy's family were landowners. Viola's mother was a strong and wise but an emotionally cold woman, having been orphaned at the age of four and shuttled between relatives growing up. Viola's father was a timid and fearful man who allowed his wife to run the show. The family suffered a harsh, difficult life of scarcity that was common to their poor station.

Viola was the youngest of four with three older brothers. She was a natural beauty with a china-white complexion and although they revered her they never showed her much love. Growing up, it seemed that all I heard about was my grandmother's beauty.

Viola married my charming grandfather, Roy, in 1931, and they leased an apple farm to work and live on. But those were the early years of the Dust Bowl and Great Depression, and they could not succeed. The combination of these two devastating situations was emotionally scaring for my anxious grandmother. She told me stories about how frightened she felt. She talked about how the insidious dust was in everything and that no one had money. She said men came to their back door asking for food and that loaves of bread and entire bushels of apples cost only ten cents each.

Viola and Roy had married in their early twenties, which was considered "over the hill" in the farming community where most people married in their late teens. They struggled to get pregnant but after waiting four long years my mother was born in 1935. Like many children who are desperately desired, my mother was their treasure and, according to her, they were excellent parents.

Any time I saw my grandmother, she told me what a beautiful and contented child my mother had been and how she charmed anyone she met. As my mother got older, her musical talent and academic accomplishments made her even more remarkable to my grandmother. I don't think my grandmother could really believe that my mother was her child. Looking back now, it is clear to me that my grandmother idolized my mother.

My grandfather Roy was the only person in his family to attend college. Educated as a geologist, he was able to leave farming and go to work in the oil industry when things didn't work out with the apple farm.

He traveled for his job and the family moved throughout the Midwest to a new town every two years until 1949 when they settled down in Denver so that my mother could attend high school. My mother and grandmother grew very close from moving around the country. They relied on each other for company when my grandfather was away and were each other's only friend each time they moved to a new town.

My memory of my grandfather Roy was that he was a "man's man" who could fix anything and that he was a loving, generous guy who helped his neighbors. He was jovial and fun. If asked his favorite pastime he would have said it was to drink and play cards with "the boys." In contrast, my grandmother Viola was high-strung and difficult to be around. Something was always bothering her and she never seemed content. To me she was persnickety and difficult complaining often with an irritable nature. She was a vain little lady who spent hours in front of the mirror "doing her face." The hyperfocus on her external beauty, without a foundation of love from her childhood, meant an emotional imbalance had been created that lasted throughout her lifetime. However people seemed to overlook her rude, entitled, and demanding behavior because of her looks. There was a stark contrast between my grandparents. While my grandfather saw life through a lens of fun and love, my grandmother saw life through a lens of fear and negativity.

. . .

Throughout my childhood, when we visited my grandparents in Denver, I would be trapped in my grandmother's company for hours at a time. She would brag about my mother incessantly. She would tell me stories about how my mother quoted Bible verse when she was four and played the piano from the age of five.

Because she never had anything nice to say to me or about me, her gushing commentary about my mother hurt and chipped away at my self-esteem. I felt shamefully inadequate for not being good enough. One afternoon, when I was about ten, I remember happily running across the street to see her. When I got there she gave me a disapproving look and said, "Lisa, you run like a truck driver. You should act more like a girl."

No one ever witnessed the critical things my grandmother said or the unkind way she treated me, but by the time I was in the third or fourth grade, it started to sink in. Even though I saw her only twice a year, she was ever-present in our family discussions, which made her messages to me very powerful. It compounded the negativity I was also experiencing at home and in school at that time. As a result, I felt like I didn't fit in anywhere.

Whenever I tried to talk to my mother about my grandmother's behavior or tell her something she had said that hurt my feelings, my mother would brush it off and dismiss it, saying, "No she didn't," or, "She was always a good mother to me." Then she would change the subject. Her confident, dismissive response confused me. I knew what I felt was legitimate but I was told it was wrong. This became the root of the "crazy-making" I would experience from my mother's and other people's denial regarding the emotional difficulties I had throughout my childhood.

The most important person in my life (my mother), was supposed to understand me, protect me, and take care of me. Instead, she told me that what I was feeling was wrong—denying what I intuitively knew to be true. I felt lost and alone. At that time I only knew to look outside of myself for validation and the messages I received were not at all helpful.

My mother and I were very different. I experienced life in extreme ways and "took things hard" while my mother was more easygoing and moderate. She did not have the emotional awareness nor the skill set to handle my complex and sensitive personality. Instead of helping me to understand what I was experiencing, she would ignore or deny things she found uncomfortable or unanswerable.

My mother is a fixer. She didn't have the emotional education to just listen to me without 'solving' the problem. What I needed was for her to say things like, 'That must have really hurt," or "Tell me more," or "Oh? Really?" This way I would have been encouraged to continue sharing my feelings until I was finished. Knowing I was being heard and supported would have provided validation and help to build my self-esteem.

My mother and I have talked about this recently and she said felt like she would be disrespecting her mother if she acknowledged or validated or supported me. Her loyalty was to her mother. She was also not one to make waves or confront anything. But because she denied her mother's bad behavior to me I felt as if I'd been thrown under the bus. It wouldn't have changed my grandmother's behavior had my mother validated my experience, but I would have felt seen, heard, loved, and supported, and made to feel like I mattered.

In glaring contrast to my relationship with my grandmother, my grandfather and my brother were the best of friends and thoroughly enjoyed each other's company. They shared common interests, and my brother credits our grandfather with being a more important and positive male role model for him than our father throughout our school-age years.

I was never invited to spend much time with this cool man that everyone seemed to love. My grandfather was nice to me and called me Lisa Belle, but he seemed to be only interested in my brother. I wanted to be included but, as a girl, it was never an option. At that time, the boys went with the men, and the girls went with the women, regardless of interest. So I watched my brother and grandfather from a distance and felt an odd imbalance. I was unable to identify or understand why I felt so badly and no one else seemed to notice.

While it may seem minor that my feelings were never validated, these subtle, consistent messages, in combination with many other negative social experiences from others in my family and at school, led to my developing profound insecurity and low self-esteem.

The resulting damage from the accumulation of the insidious subtle slights I received from all facets of my life instilled in me a profound self-doubt and self-loathing that would warp my perception of how I received and processed my life experiences and social information up and through 9/11.

•   •   •

NEIL AND CONNIE

My parents met on a blind date in 1955, their sophomore year at Colorado A&M (now Colorado State University). A romantic at heart, my father fell in love at first sight. On their first date, he was so mesmerized by my mother that, after dropping her off, he lit a cigarette as he drove away and absentmindedly threw the car lighter out the window. He never found it again.

My mother was one of three girls from her high school class who attended college and the only one who graduated four years later. She studied occupational therapy, a new and upcoming field in the 1950s having been encouraged by her mother to train in a useful vocation in case she ever needed to rely on herself. True to form as someone who has a knack for being in the right place at the right time, my mother was a maverick of her time choosing a career that would later become mainstream. When I went to college in 1978, my mother effortlessly rejoined the workforce and started a full-time occupational therapy practice that lasted for thirty years.

My parents were a beautiful couple stepping into the prime of their lives, with a bright future ahead of them. They were engaged by their senior year and married two days after graduation in June 1957.

They moved to Denver, and, ten months later, my brother Mark was born. The honeymoon pregnancy had foiled my mother's plans to build a career, but she did work for two years until she became pregnant with me.

In the spring of 1960, just months before I was born, my family left Denver and moved to New Jersey in a career change for my father, who had been hired by an advertising agency on Madison Avenue in New York.

The hit series *Mad Men* portrays the world of the advertising industry on Madison Avenue in the 1960s. When I first saw it, I thought I was watching my well-groomed father with his terse, humorless disposition. However, contrary to the image the show depicts, my father loved my mother and to my knowledge he was never a womanizer, but the portrayal of doing business over three-martini lunches was a reality for him.

The fall of 1960 should have been a joyful time for my parents with the anticipated birth of their second child (me!). But three days before I was born, my grandmother Margaret died of walking pneumonia. I believe this fatal condition developed as a result of being emotionally run-down from her second divorce, which had occurred earlier that summer. Her death derailed everyone and orphaned her youngest daughter, Marsha, who was then eleven years old.

To compound the devastation, at Margaret's funeral, my father confronted his Aunt Ruby about going into Margaret's house in the days after her death and taking antiques and artwork. Ruby vehemently denied doing so, and to my father's amazement, his grandmother Merta sided with her. The intense fight became a pivotal moment in the family. Even though Ruby and her teenage daughters had been living with Margaret, they refused to take Marsha in. Therefore, within days of Margaret's death, Marsha came to live with my parents as their third (and preteen) child. My young parents, both age twenty-five at the time, became her legal, adoptive guardians. I was born three days after Margaret's death on September 3, 1960 into a dark, chaotic, and pain-filled energy.

Because of the fight, the relationship between my father and his aunts and grandmother was completely severed. My father and his younger sisters, Judy (who was twenty-one) and Marsha, lost all contact with their mother's family and would never again reconcile with the close relatives with whom they'd grown up. I would not meet any of my father's first cousins until I was in my late twenties and the older generation had died.

The shock of Margaret's death was devastating for my father. He had never properly grieved the death of his father, and now he had to deal with the loss of his mother, the unexpected responsibility for his preteen sister, and the negative impact from his complicated, extended family experience. The joy of the arrival of his baby daughter was overshadowed by it all.

The catastrophic situation surrounding Margaret's untimely death negatively shifted the trajectory of my young family's lives forever. My father's grief and anger from so much loss and family upheaval threw him completely off balance. The sudden responsibility of having to adopt and raise his preteen sister, who was fourteen years his junior, without any emotional or financial support, was overwhelming. To top it off, he had a two-and-a-half-year-old son and a brand-new baby girl to raise. Needless to say, there was tension, turmoil, and very little joy in our household in the first weeks and months and years of my life.

Because my mother's family experience was kinder and gentler she was unequipped to handle the toxicity and struggles with the caustic and poisonous relationship with my father's family. But as his true, loving partner, she supported him in every way possible, and, together, they stepped up to the responsibility they were handed.

They both did their best for Marsha and for my brother and me, but this catastrophe was far beyond their emotional and psychological capacity. Not only were they alone in the situation, but also because they were so young they lacked the wisdom and maturity of life experience to guide them. In addition, at that time in society, there was little emotional education or understanding of the nuances of navigating complex relationships.

Although my father may have confided in a few older male friends, he never sought any type of professional help. To my knowledge, he did not let his guard down nor share his feelings with anyone but my mother. He never went to church with our family as he made it pretty clear he was very angry with God. He sadly lacked any soulful or healthy expression to relieve his pain—so, instead, he drank.

Because of the lack of emotional awareness and limited expression of grief that was acceptable by society then, my family's emotional damage and dysfunction began to build and expand with the pressure going sideways, hot and fast, like the steam when a lid is placed on a pot of boiling water.

My grandmother Margaret's untimely death and all it brought with it set the tone for my future where the subtle slights from the people closest to me, and the world around me, would fester and swell. A future where a growing sense of not feeling seen, heard, or understood would shape and create my perception of how I viewed myself and how I fit into the world.

●　●　●

MARSHA

I was a newborn, and my brother was a toddler when my Aunt Marsha came to live with us. It is hard to imagine how sad and heartbreaking her experience must have been.

She had been an infant when her father Milton died. The two alcoholic stepfathers that followed surely made her life unstable and difficult. To then lose her mother so suddenly and also become estranged from her same-aged cousins, Aunt Ruby, and her grandmother within days of her mother's death must have been as confusing as it was excruciating. It is easy to understand how her view of the world through her life's lens could have been badly warped and refracted.

Marsha was closer in age to my brother and me (by nine and eleven years) than she was to my father. Marsha loved my sweet brother, Mark, but as I grew up she treated me as if she were another parent, chastising and scolding me for the slightest infraction. In my need to be loved, I remember trying hard to please her, but she never seemed interested. I watched as Marsha played with Mark, showering him with affection. However, from my earliest memories, I remember feeling left out and excluded by her.

Years later, when I spoke to Dr. VK about this, she said that it was probably because I was emotionally needy and another female in the household; Marsha was most likely envious, even though I was so little (I was six when Marsha left for college). As much as being shunned by Marsha hurt me and added to my feelings of alienation, I can understand it happening, given the level of trauma and tragedy she experienced in her young life. But the subtle and not-so-subtle slights I received from her further helped to undercut my young, developing self-esteem.

• • •

Marsha went to high school and college throughout the 1960s, which brought the unpopular Viet Nam War and the Civil Rights and Feminist Movements right to our front door.

I remember playing in the mornings in front of our black-and-white television in the living room. After the children's programming ended, Hugh Downs and Barbara Walters would come on *The Today Show* and report stories of the social disruption plaguing the country. They would show death-toll maps from the war in Viet Nam.

As things escalated, the news reported protest riots on college campuses across the country. My father was furious when they burned a building at his alma mater, Colorado State University. As a young child, all I saw was his anger. I didn't understand what was happening. He was so upset, I remember thinking that it might be the end of the world.

By the late 1960s, the politics of the Viet Nam War, and the resulting social turbulence and perceived disrespect of the younger generation (Marsha's) had pushed my father's anger to outrage. He yelled and ranted about these situations nightly at the dinner table. I would learn later in therapy that this might have been a refraction of his compassion for the horrible situation we were in. I believe his fury was magnified by his fear and frustration at being so powerless to change what was going on around him.

My intense and sensitive father was heartbroken over the boys he knew from the community who'd been killed in Viet Nam. He had sad memories from his childhood during World War II of seeing gold stars in the windows of his neighbor's houses whose fathers, sons, and brothers had been killed in action.

Death and loss were unprocessed dark holes for my father and he didn't have a healthy outlet for these powerful emotions. Unfortunately, society didn't have any answers then, either.

An activist by nature, on college breaks Marsha brought home the radical, new thinking from the liberal social movements. The argumentative conflict that had always existed between her and my father intensified and created incredible negative energy. My father's views were aligned with the traditional, conservative establishment thinking of his generation. Like many children who experience intense anger in their households, I blamed myself thinking that I had done something wrong. The dark intensity of being around them left me feeling anxious and isolated. They were both powerful and angry; they were seldom nice to each other. It also seemed that they were rarely nice to me, either.

As they fought, my mother would sit silently and listen. She admitted that she did not engage with them because she recognized their powerful energies and knew she would not be heard. I know they both respected her, and they might have listened to her if she had tried. I don't remember her saying much to Marsha, and she never spoke up against my father throughout my childhood except for an occasional, "Now, Neil . . ."

.   .   .

My mother and my brother Mark were nice and kind, and they did love me. However, their sweet, quiet energy was not remotely as powerful as my older-sister-aunt's and my father's negative, hostile energy. Why wasn't the love of my mother and brother enough to offset this? Why do negative experiences carry so much more weight than positive?

I was social and outgoing compared to my brother, who was quiet and hesitant. I was also headstrong and curious with a lot of energy. Although two years older, Mark let me try things first. We got along well because we were so different. He was sweet and loving and tried to take care of me. His reserved, obedient nature was rewarded in my family, while my loud and busy behavior was reprimanded. He was better at staying in the background while I jumped in with both feet. It comes as no surprise that I was often in trouble, and he became the favored child.

The world did not distinguish between behavior and the person then. It was *You are a bad girl*—not that the bad behavior is bad. And I got the message loud and clear.

.   .   .

I know now that my sensitivity about being excluded from relationships began in early childhood. Because of the consistent subtle slights I received from my close family members from a very early age, and the lack of positive information to counter the subtle negative messages, my emotional foundation was shaky and unstable creating a warped lens through which I viewed my life.

I can recall things from my childhood in intricate detail: what I wore, places we went, and things that were said. I remember I wore a red plaid jumper with a white blouse and new brown leather shoes on my first day of school in second grade. I remember every make, model, and color car we ever owned. I remember getting on the ski lift with my dad when I was five and watching JFKs funeral when I was three. It's hard to heal when you cannot forget even the smallest details.

From my acute perception and memory, I began to create stories that I would tell myself about my world and my place in it. No one filled the void with positive or correct information to counter what I was telling myself, therefore, as I grew older those negative stories became my truth.

• • •

LISA–CHILDHOOD YEARS

Looking from the outside in, my household resembled the families in the 1950s and 1960s television shows *Father Knows Best* or *Leave It to Beaver.* The terse and serious father figure gave all-knowing, wise counsel, while the sweet and compliant mother stayed in the background, supportively smiling and nodding her head. The only difference at my house was that my mother didn't wear aprons or do housework in a dress and high heels.

I looked up to my father, who was a powerful patriarch with high intelligence and a visionary gift. He was handsome and charming and could sometimes be great, but most often, he was distant and moody, with a hair-trigger temper.

But when he was warm and "present" and you were caught in the glow of his loving attention, there was no better place to be. My father had a magnetic energy that was completely engaging. However like many men of his generation, he also radiated a repelling energy and always seemed too busy to be interrupted. He said to me years later that children only became interesting to him after the age of twelve.

From his experience as an adman on Madison Avenue, he had a creative vision and left New York to open his own marketing consulting firm in 1967; it was then that we moved to coastal New Jersey. He was quickly successful, but the stress of growing and managing his company left him terse and intolerant. He was serious and humorless most of the time. He seemed lost in thought even when he was cutting the grass or doing chores. His only recreation was fishing, but that was an isolated activity.

My mother was nice and sweet and pretty, and I loved her. I wanted to be just like her. I would come to learn that my personality was inherently like my father's, and that my learned behavior came from my mother; needless to say, the two did not mesh. I tried so hard to be like my mother but it was like putting a square peg in a round hole.

As patient as she was, though, I often exasperated her. I would blow through the door after school, like a whirling dervish, asking to do a million things that required her time and attention. She would scold me then, calling me "a pill" and tell me to stop running her life.

In her sweetness, I see now that my mother was trying to offset the negativity from my father. She couldn't change him or manage his behavior so my mother overserved love and kindness to make up for my father's anger and emotional distance. Their marriage and our family life looked like the textbook version of what society dictated in the 1950s and 1960s. But by her ignoring the complex emotional issues, which intensified over time, another layer within our family dysfunction was created.

As we've talked over the years, my mother told me she never had a problem with her role. She liked the gender-role stereotypic structure they had and was never unhappy being a supportive wife, homemaker, and mother. As a contented rule-follower, she followed the rules set by society, which, for all intents and purposes, should have worked. She happily stayed on the surface, swept damage and difficulty under the rug, and wrapped everything up in a nice, neat package just like the thirty-minute sitcoms we watched on television.

Even though I felt deeply and struggled with my experiences, I was a naturally happy child who loved to play. I was effervescent and charming but I could also be difficult and oppositional if there was something I did not want to do or if things didn't go my way. I could be demanding and had a strong personality like the adults around me. I was a complex character from an early age.

Due to my family experience in early childhood, by the time I went to school, I was filled with anxiety, self-doubt, and a lack of understanding of who I was and desperately wanted to be accepted, loved, and included. This set me up for a disastrous social experience in school.

•   •   •

LISA—ELEMENTARY AND MIDDLE SCHOOL YEARS

I was seven and in the second grade in 1967 when we moved to a new town and a new school. Today I would probably be diagnosed with learning disabilities. I was also young for my grade. These two things combined with the anxiety from my life at home meant that I couldn't stop talking. I was in trouble all the time in school, too. Even at age seven, I still sucked my thumb to comfort myself. For this, I was continually scolded and shamed by the teacher.

By the end of most days, my teacher had pushed my desk all the way to the back of the classroom, away from my class-mates. At recess, all the classes came together, but, as we ran around on the playground, I sensed I was being shunned and left out by many of the kids. Was this true or was I paranoid from my family training?

I struggled and managed until fifth grade when I was caught picking my nose in science class while absentmindedly watching a filmstrip. The mean girls saw me do it, and, from that moment on, I never lived it down. The news spread like wildfire. I was ostracized, mocked, and bullied unmercifully by the majority of the kids in my grade, as the adults and teachers looked the other way. Being hit by these not-so-subtle slights felt like I was being beaten. Because I knew I was guilty I shamed and punished myself, too, becoming a doormat for them to step on.

I was too ashamed to tell my mother what was happening, and I would never tell my father. By then it was also clear that my mother could not or would not help me, and because my father was so reactive and explosive, telling him would have only made things worse. So I was in it alone.

By middle school, the tone was set for my social future in this upper-middle class community, where it seemed that the norm for both adults and children was to look condescendingly down their noses at others. Once you were pigeonholed with a reputation, you were stuck there forever.

In contrast to my experience, my mother was pretty and popular and very high achieving. She was the president of the PTA when I was in grammar school and the president of the Junior League when I was in junior high. She was the first woman elected to the Board of Education for our regional high school in 1974. This was all great except for the fact that her social successes made my social failure even more glaring.

My mother could not relate to me nor understand what my life was like. When I tried to explain how I felt about things that would happen in the family or in school she would tell me I was being too sensitive. She seemed to lack the inherent awareness to sense what was happening to me. Years later, she told me she never knew what was happening because I was such a good actress. As hard as that was to hear, I see now that it was probably true.

On the rare occasion when I would tell her about being teased she'd say something like, "Oh, Lisa—no they're not. Everyone likes you." Then she would change the subject. This happened so often that I didn't tell her anything for a long time. Her lack of support continued to erode my already unstable emotional foundation.

One time in seventh grade, when I was feeling really low, I again risked confiding in my mother about how much I was being teased. She said, "Oh, just tell them they're being immature."

The next day when I tried this, it gave the kids new fuel to mock me further. They called me "Miss Maturity" for the next three months, in addition to whispering, pointing at me, and giggling.

So by the end of middle school I was trapped in this awful place where no one would come near me or risk his or her reputation by showing me any understanding or kindness.

As hard as I would try to fit in (also a problem), everything seemed to backfire. I created for myself an experiential loop and a self-fulfilling prophecy based on my negative experiences. In my rumination I repeated over and over the mean and nasty stories I heard from others and made up about myself. Soon I became my own worst enemy. It is true that we gravitate to what is familiar, even when it is negative.

It was the late 1960s and early 1970s then, and my father was struggling in business. I would watch him refill his glass with gin three or four times during dinner then my brother and I would be subjected to his alcoholic rants. He yelled so loudly and viciously that it felt as if we were being beaten. He would stop only when we were both in tears, and then he would shame us for crying. At that point, we would leave the table and escape to our rooms.

I was too young to understand that my father's anger was fed by his own deficiencies, frustrations, and alcohol and that he was using the dinner table as the boardroom where he was Commander-in-Chief, and always right.

When my mother came upstairs to tuck me in, she would tell me that my father loved me and try to explain his angry outbursts. She would say that he was angry at the world, but I didn't understand what she meant. Maybe if she had said, "Lisa, you didn't deserve that, you didn't do anything wrong," I would have felt more supported, but she would not speak out against him. As a child, I could not comprehend that the yelling wasn't because of me because I was in trouble so much of the time.

• • •

My brother, Mark, and I were good friends growing up. We were so different that we never competed. Besides getting along well we were also unified in the experience of our father as our common enemy.

We lived at the end of a dead-end street with a lot of space between the houses. There were very few kids and no neighborhood to speak of. Of the few girls my age, none of them lived near by and I would have to ride my bike down several long streets to get to their houses. But because we weren't really friends my attempts to play with them dwindled quickly. By the end of fifth grade, I was isolated and alone.

My brother's experience was different. He had three close friends right up the street. We lived on the water and when my brother turned twelve, my father let him use our little skiff to go out on the river with his friends. They rode bikes back and forth to each other's houses every day after school. They explored the beaches and islands in the river and lived a remarkable "boy's life."

Things got really bad for me in sixth grade and I needed Mark to stand up for me against the bullies at school but I knew that it wasn't in his nature to do so. Instead, he took care of me by allowing me to hang out with him and his friends. In addition to roaming the waterways and countryside, the boys started building things out of driftwood and bags of nails. In junior high, they built a two-story tree house; in high school, they built a "hut" on pilings over the muddy beach in our backyard. As a result, our house was the place to be. They had legendary parties throughout high school and I was welcomed and included as one of the "original gang."

Mark's friends were like older brothers to me. Because I was so sad and lonely, I was extraordinarily grateful for their kindness and friendship, and I made a point to never be a pest or annoying in any way. By the time they left for college when I was sixteen, they were each personal friends of mine, too. I don't know if I would be here today if it wasn't for the decency of those boys.

Even with the kindness of my brother and his friends, the power of the bullying I was experiencing at school was so severe that it dominated my life. In spite of them, I still felt unprotected from aggressors and had few girlfriends or adults in my life to offset the effects it had on me.

In spite of their kindness, it wasn't enough and I was still desperately insecure, painfully lonely, and very sad. From being unseen, unheard, and unacknowledged, I was needy and starved for attention. Without understanding the concept then, I was suffering from depression. By junior high school I thought about suicide often but never did it because I didn't want to hurt my mother.

．　．　．

LISA–THE HIGH SCHOOL YEARS

When I got to high school, things improved a bit as a second town of kids blended in. Everyone was a little older and more mature, and the distractions were greater. But by then, my self-esteem had been crushed.

In grammar school, I'd started to have hateful, vengeful mental rumination. I'd think, *You are so ugly and fat. Why are you such a loser? You can't do anything right.* It picked up steam as I entered puberty and my adolescent hormones kicked in. I felt like even more of a social outlier from my refracted point of view. I could not break free of my ever-present, insecure, self-loathing paranoia; I hated myself from the depths of my soul.

I desperately wanted to be a cheerleader, so against my better judgment, I went out for the highly competitive squad. Because I can project my voice and do a decent cartwheel, I made the team. Who was also on the squad? That's right—my nemeses—the same tormentors from grammar school. I set myself up to be in their company every day after school and all day Saturdays at football games. In the winter, we switched to basketball, with practices after school and evening games. I willingly chose to spend my free time with these horrible girls.

What was I thinking? Why did I knowingly throw myself into that snake pit? I think because somewhere deep down I knew that I was just as good as they were. I wanted to fight back, but I didn't because I knew that no one would back me up, and I would be left in an even worse position. I see now that I was testing myself. It took strength and courage to withstand the situation I had put myself in and my warrior-self was making her appearance. The drive and challenge to be a cheerleader was worth the price. I would stand there and take it, not backing down but not fighting back, either—something I regretted for years.

. . .

Because the legal drinking age in New Jersey in the 1970s was eighteen, we all drank in bars in high school. I lived in a beach community on the Jersey Shore, with dozens of bars along the strip. Being carded was a joke, and driving drunk was a sport.

By the end of high school, I had made friends with the other social outliers in my grade, many of whom became some of the most interesting adults out of our graduating class. We all joined in the party scene becoming skilled drinkers because drinking was a way to fit in. I was naturally good at it—I could hold my liquor and never got sick, possibly because I have the drinking gene on both sides of my family.

We all drank. Our parents drank. And our parents looked the other away. "Out of sight, out of mind" was the operative parental stance then. Maybe that's why we are such helicopter parents with our children today; we know how close we came to the edge.

I thought I was fooling people. When I was drinking, I could repress my low self-esteem and deep insecurities with self-deprecating humor and being a fun drunk. But when I was sober, I was still so desperate and self-loathing that most of my sentences started with "I'm sorry."

In the fall of 1976, after my brother left for college, my parents started looking for a new place to live. It was the beginning of my junior year. They left most weekends in my last two years of high school to look at towns up and down the east coast. I stayed by myself, took care of the dogs, and watched the house.

My father had checked out on parenting by then. He was done. With my brother gone, my father wanted out of New Jersey but was forced to unhappily bide his time until I graduated. He was very dark and became even more unpleasant in my last years of high school. By the time I went to college, my father was more than ready to see me go.

My light had almost been extinguished by the time I graduated from high school. My experience of the world and the people in it—my close family members, the teachers and kids at school, the community I lived in—was universal: no one was nice. I tried to be nice and love enough for everyone, but it pushed people further away. Thank God my brother and mother didn't add to my difficulties. Had one more thing happened, I might not be here today.

• • •

LISA–THE COLLEGE YEARS

At my parents' suggestion, I went west to college, attending their alma mater, Colorado State University (CSU). My grandfather Roy had died the year before, and they thought that having me closer to Viola in Denver would be good for us both. In truth, I think they saw it as a chance to be relieved of some of the responsibility of caring for my difficult grandmother. Although we never discussed it in detail, they also perceived the West to be a kinder, gentler nation, and that getting me out of the caustic Northeast would be a good thing.

To guide me, my father told me I could go to school anywhere except the Northeast or Boulder, but, for some reason, we never made trips to look at other colleges.

So I was indirectly directed to go to CSU. It seemed logical to me since I had heard about it for my entire life and had visited Denver many times. I was accepted in the fall of 1977. When my parents had gone to Fort Collins and Colorado A&M, the enrollment was 4,000 undergraduates; when I went, it was 18,000 and was on a completely different campus.

Even though I knew Colorado well, when I arrived at CSU, I might as well have landed on a different planet. I was in complete culture shock. Having left the preppy, snotty Northeast, I landed smack in the middle of the country and a different world. The majority of students came from the central part of the country: Ohio, Indiana, Illinois, Iowa, Utah, Arizona, Kansas, Nebraska, Texas, but very few from the Northeast or West Coast.

My father's plan had worked. I had gotten out of the Northeast, but now I was a fish out of water. There I was with my Faire Isle sweaters, plaid kilts, knee socks, and clogs—along with all of my emotional baggage—while the other kids were wearing rodeo belts, cowboy boots, hats, and Wrangler jeans. They looked at me like I was from outer space. But, people there were much kinder. They politely smiled and said "Hello" in passing; they accepted me in all my weirdness—a welcome change from people back home.

In college, my insecurity and self-loathing were well entrenched, but my outgoing nature and social camouflaging skills carried me through. I had learned well from my mother's teachings to put on a happy face, but inside I was struggling and sad.

A few weeks into school, someone asked me, "Why are you so mean?" I thought, *Me? Mean? Impossible. I'm not mean. I'm funny.* They were referring to my sarcastic East Coast sense of humor. I learned quickly that sarcasm isn't funny–that it is rooted in thinly veiled anger based on cruelty and at someone else's expense. Sarcasm comes from people who are insecure about themselves. I didn't mean to do it, but it had meant survival at home; in this new world, it was never my intention to be hurtful, so I quickly stopped.

Many people my age would agree that, in the late 1970s, when we left for college, our parents were happy to see us go. Jokingly, the operative phrase would be, "Don't let the door hit you on the way out."

We were allowed to be very independent—probably too much so—but, as we didn't know any better, we accepted it. Although the thought of leaving home was terrifying, the freedom of it offered an intrepid intrigue. So we forged ahead, as eighteen-year-old young adults, setting off to explore the world and make mistakes on our own terms.

My parents cut me loose and moved from my hometown in New Jersey to a remote town on the eastern shore of the Chesapeake Bay the first summer I was in college. I spent my vacations, except for Christmas and summers, with my grandmother Viola.

My father had an investment condo near my hometown that he had been using as an office, so I lived there during my summers in college. I commuted to New York for my internships and was close to the beach and my friends. I would see my parents some weekends, but, for the most part, I was on my own.

●   ●   ●

LISA–THE TWENTIES AND TED LUCKETT

My years in Colorado softened me, and I made lifelong friends in college. But deep down inside, even if people were nice or seemed to like me, I didn't really believe them. In my heart, I was still unlovable, flawed, and undeserving; I always felt like an outlier.

I carried with me the deep self-loathing and personality disorders from my painful childhood. I brought my sad, insecure inner child with me into every relationship and interaction I had. I didn't know what it meant to be nice to myself or that it was even allowed.

I landed a job selling advertising for a plastics magazine before graduation and moved to Denver instead of heading back to New York as I had always planned.

Now in my early twenties, I continued to struggle with friends and have relationship issues, but I pushed ahead in business with the drive and ambition I had learned from my father at the dinner table. I found early success in radio advertising sales in Denver, a perfect vocation for the neurotic and insecure.

In the spring of 1985, when I was twenty four years old, I moved back to the East Coast. I was unprepared for New York, just as I had been unprepared when I had arrived at CSU. I thought I knew what I was getting into because of my summer internship, but again the (reverse) culture shock was brutal. I only had one friend from high school with whom I'd stayed in touch, and she was busy with her own established life. I struggled with roommates and was evicted from my first apartment within six months of arriving. I didn't have nearly enough money, and I was very, very lonely.

Doing business in New York, the number-one radio market in the country, was night and day from Denver. It was competitive and cutthroat, and I was the eighteenth salesperson on a staff of eighteen. By the fall of 1985, six months after I started, I was in financial ruins from a series of commission charge-backs from advertisers who had filed for Chapter 11 bankruptcy.

I picked myself up from the bottom when I started doing aerobics at a Living Well Lady workout studio that was near my apartment. I had bought a membership in Denver that transferred to New York so exercise became my free entertainment. In the mid-1980s certification to teach was not yet required, so I soon became a high-impact aerobics instructor, teaching classes after work. I also got a job on the weekends at a high-end men's clothing store on the Upper East Side to help make ends meet. The endorphins from exercise and the empowerment from proactively taking steps to get myself out of the hole helped to set me on a positive new course.

By the end of 1986, I crawled back from the depths of financial despair in a rags-to-riches comeback, winning Salesperson of the Year after a lucrative and creative sale made to the Observation Deck at the World Trade Center. (Yup, that's right.)

Three weeks before the award was announced, I started dating this cute guy named Ted. So, not only did I win money and remarkable recognition from one of the top radio stations in the country, but the Universe also awarded me Teddy Luckett as the ultimate prize of my life.

Although my self-loathing was still ever-present, achieving this recognition in my hard-fought career allowed me to feel my first true sense of self-confidence. By making it through the social and financial struggles of those early years in New York, I had learned my first lesson in self-love. Had I met Teddy any earlier, I might have sabotaged the relationship due to my low self-esteem and feelings of worthlessness. But this time, my inner voice said firmly, "*Stop it, Lisa. You deserve this.*" I chose to give myself permission, leaned in, and fell head over heels in love with my soul mate and the man of my dreams.

Everyone loved Teddy Luckett. Initially I thought, "*What is wrong with this guy that he would want me?*" As much as I debated it internally, a grain of self-value allowed me to believe there must be something worthy within me if I was the one he was choosing. Winning the sales award had elevated me to a brand-new place and allowed me to take a huge step forward in personal growth and self-esteem.

Because Ted was naturally easygoing, I became softer. Being in love and supported by someone who loves you back will do that. Being around his lighthearted humor and playful, gentle demeanor brought out those traits in me. He was genuinely kind, open, and generous in showing love. I had to constantly remind myself that I was worth it, that I deserved it. I learned to roll with things just by being around him. I let go and allowed myself to accept the wondrous gift of being loved by this incredible man.

Being with Ted gave me the social acceptance I had always wanted. Because he was so well loved, the people who loved him loved me without hesitation. His college friends from Ohio Wesleyan University were immediately accepting, warm, and inclusive. The sailing community he grew up with in Westchester County, New York, welcomed me with open arms.

Unfortunately, Ted's family did not. They were not happy about me. Ted's denial of their behavior toward me was the only dark cloud in our relationship. It was closely reminiscent of my mother's denial of the behavior of my family members and peer groups throughout my childhood, which brought my childhood pain back to the surface.

But that aside, Ted and I were a great team. He was the yin to my yang as I was to him. We were better together than we were apart. He rounded off my sharp edges and I helped to motivate him. We entertained our clients together and thrived as yuppies in the late 1980s with Ted on Wall Street and me in radio advertising.

We were outgoing and social, which meant we did a lot of drinking. It was the sign of the times. Having been raised in the late '70s and '80s, we were varsity partiers and had a great time together with our friends and clients—moving, shaking, and living the materialistic 1980s dream.

Ted had grown up sailing. By the time I met him, he had reached the top levels of the sport, crewing on elite racing boats. He sailed in many long-distance, offshore races, the pinnacle of which was the Bermuda Race. The race is held every other summer in June, and leaves from Newport, Rhode Island, for an 800-mile, open-ocean race to Bermuda.

At the race's finish sailors gather at the Royal Bermuda Yacht Club. There they celebrate with the club's signature drink—the Dark & Stormy, made with Gosling's Dark Rum (unique to Bermuda) and ginger beer with lime.

From the moment we met, Ted and I adopted Dark & Stormies as our own. We became known for Dark & Stormy parties both in New York and later, when we moved to New Jersey. I even served them at several memorial services held for Ted in fall after 9/11.

After a four-year courtship, Ted and I finally married in October of 1990. We were over the moon with happiness. It was so easy and simple after waiting so long. I joke that it was the longest sale of my career, but the wait was worth it.

THERAPY THE FIRST TIME

Two years after Ted and I were married, I ended up seeing a therapist on the Upper West Side of Manhattan named Laura S.

Both my brother and I were married in the fall of 1990, our weddings taking place three weeks apart, on opposite coasts in Maryland and Seattle. Now in the second year of my marriage, my mother was dumping her neediness and misery over my father's alcoholism onto me, and it was draining me of my newlywed bliss.

I had come to the realization that my father was an alcoholic when I went to college. I confronted my mother and brother about it when I came home one Christmas. They initially denied it not wanting to see the truth. We then spent the next ten years talking about him behind his back, but no one ever confronted him. As the years went by, my mother would complain about his behavior expecting my counsel, but never taking steps to change anything. I felt badly for her and could hear how unhappy she was but I was out of the house, tired of the conversation, and felt the problem was hers to handle. I had always wanted an intervention with my father but neither my mother nor my brother could do it. Now that Ted and I were finally married, I had found the happiness and joy I had been looking for all my life, and I was determined to hold onto it.

It was Thanksgiving the second year of Mark's and my new marriages and my parents had come to New York for the holiday weekend. My mother walked in and announced that Mark and his wife would not be coming East for Christmas. My mother and father would be alone for the first time, and she was beside herself. An assumption had been made that Mark and I would alternate years to be home with my parents for Christmas. Ted and I had been with them the first year, and we would be going to see his family this time; now, although it was his year, Mark was not coming.

That Saturday night, my mother and I went for a walk after dinner. She continued to whine and complain about being alone for Christmas. When I couldn't take anymore I snapped and said, "How can you dump this on me? You were never there for me when I needed you. What do you want from me now?"

This came out of the blue but once the floodgates were open, there was no going back. We circled the block at least ten times as I laid out years of pain and resentment caused by her denial of my needs and experiences. While she did listen, she didn't really respond to what I was saying. It was the first time she had ever heard it and it was so big and so deep that I don't think she knew what to say.

When my parents left the next day, I knew something had to change.

A trusted friend and coworker, who managed a crazy family life with similar issues to mine, had seen several therapists in

New York. He suggested I speak to a woman named Laura S as he felt she and I would be a good match.

The next week when I met with Laura S, I said, "I'm here to get my father to stop drinking, because my mother is driving me crazy."

Once I started telling my story, it was like releasing a dam. There was so much repressed rage and emotion that I spewed for an hour, hardly taking a breath. Thinking back on it, I picture Laura in my mind's eye, her hair blowing back, holding on for dear life trying not to be blown out of her chair.

When the hour was up, in her quiet, thoughtful way, Laura said these important words: "Well, I can't do anything about your father's drinking, but I can tell you this: you are very angry with your mother."

And *BAM!* It was like someone flipped a switch and all the pieces fell into place. Everything shifted, and all I could see was red. I had never been allowed to be angry with my mother growing up or to separate from her like a normal teenager. From living with my father's drinking for so many years, our family dynamics had created neediness in my mother that caused her to subconsciously manipulate me to never leave her.

My father always boasted that he and my mother were a unified front. As parents, they stood together "against" my brother and me as teenagers, as if we were on opposing sides in some undeclared war. My brother and I both feared my father, who ran an unspoken, protective interference around my mother. This fear of him kept me in check and obedient until he died. I never talked back or spoke up for myself to either of my parents until after Ted died and I was in my forties.

In Laura's office that day, thirty years of pain and resentment filled me with anger unlike anything I had ever felt before. I couldn't stand the thought of my mother. Suddenly it wasn't about my father anymore; it was all about my mother. It had never dawned on me to be angry with her.

Laura helped me see that my mother was the enabler in our alcoholic family system, which turned out to be as damaging, if not more so, than the behavior of my father, who was the active drinker, because she just sat there doing nothing and never protected us. This unexpected life-altering revelation left my head spinning.

I didn't speak to my mother for several weeks after they left. From the revelation with Laura, I couldn't stand the idea of talking to her and would refuse to speak to her when she called. Finally one night, Ted made me take her call.

While barely containing my rage, I told her that I could never talk to either of them growing up because she positioned herself as perfect and never understood what I was saying. I told her I couldn't talk to my father because he was always so explosive and reactive. I learned later that when we hung up she turned to my father and said, "Lisa says she could never talk to us because I was perfect and you were always drunk."

In what would be one of the greatest ironies in my life, my father stopped drinking the next day. He did not attend Alcoholics Anonymous so he never embraced what it meant to be "sober" but he was "dry" for the next four years.

In the time I spent with Laura, I learned that the relationship between therapist and patient is very special. I know this sounds obvious but it was new to me then. Very few people admitted to seeking therapy in the 1990s, so this information was not something you picked up along the way.

I liked Laura, but we were unlikely friends. We had a connective energy from the start, and I recognized her seasoned knowledge and professional skills within our first few sessions. She was wise and kind and calm, and I trusted her.

From Laura, I gained my first understanding of grief. It happened when my beloved radio station went through a management upheaval that was so abrupt and negative the future looked bleak for all of us. My sales numbers were good so I wasn't worried about losing my job, but it had been such a good place to work that I came to her feeling lost and very sad about the change. She said simply, "Lisa, you're grieving." I had never understood what it meant to grieve. I didn't know you could grieve for something other than death. I learned from her that any type of loss can include feelings of grief: a job change, children leaving the nest, or moving to a new place.

Another fascinating insight Laura shared was the theory that anyone who does therapy affects two generations back and three generations forward. The idea that I was changing the course of future generations intrigued me.

I had an excellent experience with Laura and began to uncover who I was and how the events and people in my life had shaped me. I left after a year knowing that one day I would go back and finish.

. . .

MARRIED WITH CHILDREN

In early 1997, when our daughter Jennifer was two and a half and I was pregnant with our son Billy, we moved back to the area on the Jersey Coast where I had grown up but to a different town, a sweet little village called Fair Haven.

While I had done well in my career and had great friends whom I loved from college, my career years, and from my life with Teddy, my insecurities were still at the foundation of my emotional experiences.

Now aged thirty-seven and a suburban mother of two, the person I was on the outside did not match the one on the inside. I still suffered enormous misunderstanding, from seeing life through my refracted lens, with years of foundational self-loathing and anger at its root. This often caused my view of others to be misinterpreted and negatively skewed. I was such a damaged, sensitive soul with a strong, dominant personality that just walking into a room could cause conflict for me in my mind.

I would ruminate almost nightly, lying awake for hours, with my mind spinning through loops of anger, vengeance, and self-punishment about interactions with family members and other situations that left me feeling out of control. I felt insane, irritable, and exhausted.

In the back of my mind I also knew I shouldn't be drinking, which compounded the problem.

Leaving my career to become a full-time mother was a privileged option and one I had always dreamed of having, but when I got there, it was nothing as I had imagined.

I loved and adored my kids, but I discovered that raising children entailed a deep sense of worry and a constant fear factor that I had never previously considered. The emotional responsibility not to mess them up was always on my mind, yet, despite my concern, I seemed to be doing it anyway. As much as I wanted the Dream Date fantasy of the little house with the white picket fence, the reality of being an at-home mom was more like a ratio of 10 percent joy, 90 percent other.

By the late 1990s, as an emotionally dispirited, stressed-out mother of two, I was reaching the peak of my tolerance and needed a new focus.

In the summer of 2000, when Jen and Billy were six and three, Ted and I strategically planned his move to Cantor Fitzgerald's new subsidiary company called ESpeed, one of the first electronic trading platforms that would forever change the future of Wall Street.

Our plan was that Ted would learn to sell software, becoming more versed in the new world of technology, and we would become independent contractors job-sharing a software sales job.

I was starving for intellectual stimulation, and did not want to be a soccer mom, but Ted, ready for a break from the grind, was happy to be a soccer dad. He would be able to enjoy taking the kids to sports and attending to daily family life, and I would again be using my mind in the game of business.

•   •   •

BABY #3 THE PRE-9/11 MONTHS

I discovered I was pregnant on my fortieth birthday in September 2000, and as excited as we were about our surprise bundle of joy, our grand plan for a bright, new future flew right out the window.

A beautiful, healthy Timothy Wyatt Luckett was born in May 2001 and we were both thrilled.

But by the middle of the summer, I was a total shrew. Ted was victim to the majority of my wrath and frustration but was powerless to help me. I told him that I felt like I was drowning, but he, too, was trapped. We were at a point in our lives where we felt stuck and cornered. He was trying to make it through a job transition in this new, cutting-edge industry and did not feel secure since the company was going through significant growing pains. Leaving was not an option because we were locked into investments in the corporate partnership, so we were stuck in golden handcuffs.

Looking back, I should have been glad that Teddy did as much as he did, but the additional responsibilities that came with the third baby had put us over the edge. They say going from two children to three is like switching from man-to-man to zone defense. Once again, I was unprepared for what I was handed and, for me, being surprised is never a good thing.

I was juggling an infant and two school-age kids in three different phases of life. My workload had intensified and grown exponentially. I watched the women around me manage with happy ease and shamed myself for my frustration. Did they ever feel like I did? What was wrong with me? Why was I so unhappy?

The fantasy of motherhood had worn off. I knew I was again sidelined for another two years before my infant could communicate with me and I could feel comfortable leaving him. As money was tight, I was judicious about babysitters and brought them in only on the weekends, which meant I had long, personally unsatisfying days, very little freedom, and very little fun. I adored my kids, but it was just hard.

I chose to nurse the boys for a year, which turned out to be a mistake. Part of my resentment is that I could never hand Billy or Timmy off to Ted or anyone else to feed. I had been so guilt-ridden when I went back to work after Jen was born I decided that when the day came and I was home full-time, I would be the perfect, nurturing mother and nurse my next baby for a year. With the best of intentions, I had set myself up for a ton of frustration.

When I saw my mother after Timmy was born, she would say to me, "Lisa, you're depressed," more as an accusation than a concern. She did not offer any helpful advice, and I would not have listened if she did.

By the summer of 2001, I was overwhelmed by the constant drudgery of motherhood and could not see a light at the end of the tunnel. By late summer, without my recognizing it, I was deep in postpartum depression.

I had been tripping and bumping along in life, frustrated and confused. The misunderstandings and the relationship difficulties I was constantly facing continued to compound my warped perception of how I was supposed to fit into the world around me. I had no idea how I looked to the outside world, and I didn't know myself at all.

As I got older, my relationship with my parents had become considerably more complicated, and my anger toward them boiled right beneath the surface. Raising my kids brought back my childhood in vivid color, and my resentment grew as I gave to my children the love and attention I did not receive myself.

In my confused mind, I worried that my children would suffer the same sad life that I had. I wanted to do things differently but I could see I was making mistakes. One day when Jen was about three, I was angry with her about something and asked my friend how long I was supposed to stay mad at her. I was repeating my father's parenting of withholding love as a punishment.

My parents' behavior continued to compound my issues with them. They loved coming up to see the kids but didn't lift a finger when they were here. They came to be entertained as guests. They loved Ted. However, by the summer of 2001, they were not so sure about me.

My parents never seemed to notice how much work I was doing to manage my family, nor how much work they added by being here. I don't think it ever crossed their minds that I might need a little help, and it never crossed my mind to ask them.

In late July of 2001, my brother came back from Seattle for his twenty-fifth high school reunion. My parents came up from Maryland to see him.

The Friday afternoon of the reunion weekend, they entered the house in a flurry, said "Hello" to Jen and Billy and gave baby Timmy a kiss, then rushed out to the patio to be with my brother. They sat chatting together until Ted arrived home and cocktail hour began.

This was always Ted's moment and he happily embraced the job of amusing his in-laws. He breezed in, mixed Dark & Stormies, and became the consummate entertainer. My parents and brother loved nothing more than to bask in Ted's glow and be delighted by his charm.

I was twenty feet away and could hear their conversation clearly. The favorite topic of all four of them was boating. My brother's business in Seattle was yacht rigging, my parents had always lived on the water with boats of all kinds, and Ted was a sailor's sailor. They laughed and flattered Ted as he told stories of his glory days sailing on maxiyachts in the late '80s.

They were all having a great time while I was in the kitchen preparing dinner with steam coming out of my ears. My father could not tolerate being interrupted, so Jen and Billy gravitated back inside instead of being ignored and scolded. My mother held Timmy for a while, but I remember having all three kids with me in the hot kitchen.

Not once did anyone offer to help me. Not once did I ask for help. Not once did they shout in to include me in the conversation. Not once did I chime in. They were so swept up in the glow of the moment that if it crossed their minds to help me, they chose not to. I really don't think they were aware of me or even noticed that I was doing everything.

. . .

By the time I turned forty-one on September 3, 2001, eight days before 9/11, my experience with the adults in my family had left me bitter and resentful.

I had dutifully behaved as I had been told, toeing the line as a woman in a man's world, achieving in a high-paying career as I had been raised to do. I had married a great guy, and we had three healthy, beautiful kids and a nice house to live in, which should have made me happy. I had followed society's rules to the letter, but at that point, I was completely miserable. I felt like I was giving everything yet receiving very little in return. Everyone else was being held up and sustained, and I was drowning.

CHAPTER FOUR

UNINTENTIONALLY THROWING SHADE

The Myth of Family in Crisis

My family is a perfect example of further breaking where we were already broken. Already a generational, alcoholic system that centered on my father, my family spiraled downward from the emotional pressure caused by Teddy's death and the new fear of terrorism from the attacks on September 11, 2001.

I have a theory. I believe that when the towers fell that morning, an emotional centrifugal force began to spin that, while unseen, pushed on us with enormous negative pressure.

With this new pressure, any emotional weakness or damage we had before 9/11, was now exacerbated by the shock, fear, and terror of this unexpected, catastrophic blow. Just as a diamond will crack at its flaw when hit with a hammer, I believe that wherever we were "broken" emotionally before 9/11, we "broke" even further. If you were alcoholic, you drank more. If you did drugs, you got high more often. If you shopped for therapy, you spent more money. If you were a gambler, you risked more. If you had extramarital affairs, you cheated more. If you hovered over your children, you protected more—and the list goes on.

We used these emotional Band-Aids to soothe our troubled minds. They were salves to distract us from our fear and to numb the ache inside. However, within a few years, the centrifugal spin slowed down and our new way of life, postterrorism, was sealed over as we settled into a "new normal." But because so few people sought professional help during that time, our new normal now included deeper layers of emotional damage and painful dysfunction, with fear rooted at its foundation.

•   •   •

With the heartbreaking loss of Teddy, in the days and weeks that followed 9/11, my father's pain and anger reached an all time high. I watched him regress back to his emotionally broken, fourteen-year-old self as the long-buried grief and trauma over his father and mother's deaths resurfaced with a vengeance.

And then there is this strange numeric coincidence that dawned on me within days of Ted's death:

When my grandfather Milton died, my grandmother Margaret was forty-one years old with three children: fourteen-year-old Neil, ten-year-old Judy, and infant Marsha.

When Ted Luckett died, I was forty-one years old with three children: seven-year-old Jen, four-year-old Billy, and infant Timmy.

I believe that my father put me in his mother's place while he reverted back to his damaged and heartbroken teenage self.

* * *

By early afternoon on 9/11, my parents arrived, having driven straight up from Maryland. They walked into the human traffic jam that filled my house and were embraced with an outpouring of love and hugs by all of my friends.

I can't even imagine what their four-hour car ride was like, and we never discussed it. Both of my parents loved Ted like a son, and the bond between Ted and my father was especially tight.

I knew my dad would be beside himself. My mother, too, was devastated. In those early hours and days, everyone banded together, reeling from the shock of our losses, trying to find our footing while being completely overwhelmed by the magnitude and chaos of the event.

All day long, the television news was on. The phone rang incessantly and frazzled nerves. My house was busy and loud, filled with a frenetic energy.

By midafternoon on 9/11, I was doing my best to manage the madness. I was still functioning normally in my strange, new headspace. People were coming and going, searching for answers, making remarks in disbelief, and asking me what they could do to help. It had been five hours of pure insanity. Billy and Timmy needed normalcy, and Jen would soon be home from school.

I asked my dad to pick Jen up, which he was more than happy to do. He would take her to and from school for the week he stayed with us in New Jersey. When he went to get her, others also left to collect their own children for the afterschool hours, and my house quieted down for the first time all day.

That is except for the phone, which became an appendage to my body. Call waiting beeped through constantly; this lasted for three straight months. I actually shortened a ligament in my left shoulder from holding the phone to my ear while nursing Timmy.

In the days that followed, my mother took on the primary responsibility for Timmy. Friends traded off entertaining Billy throughout the day, away from the television and adult conversation. People arrived with food, gifts, flowers, sometimes staying for minutes and sometimes staying for hours.

The amount of food that came into my house was staggering. Within days, there was not an inch of room in the refrigerator, freezer, or space on my pantry shelf. It was really nice to not have to prepare food. One less thing to manage.

• • •

I continued my open-door policy, allowing access into my world. I sensed that people needed to see me and touch me to be reassured that, if they were ever in my situation, they, too, would be okay.

But within a few days, the chaos began to wear heavily on my parents. They wandered around the house and seemed lost. I could feel my father's agitation and my mother' confusion. They made little proactive effort to be helpful or supportive. They made comments to me about having so many people around. My mother asked annoying questions about how I was handling things and I could sense my father's gruffness and impatience escalating.

They did not understand the enlightened experience that I was having nor how I knew to let people in to help me. I was in full-function mode, awash in the moment, managing my shock and disbelief and that of everyone around me; I didn't have the time or patience to explain it to my parents. I don't think they would have understood it if I had tried. Theirs was a mind-set from another place and time. As those first days passed, I watched as they pulled in and Ted's death became about them.

THE MYTH OF FAMILY IN CRISIS

In the course of daily conversation, people would ask me how my parents were doing. People assumed that, because my parents were staying with me, they were caring for me. This is the magical thinking around family during tragedy.

I know my parents felt they were helping just by showing up. But as time went on, it was actually quite the opposite. As much as my mother thought she was taking care of Timmy, she seemed hesitant and unsure about everything. I needed her to step up and take charge of him but instead she constantly asked me about small and insignificant details of what to do or where things went. As the days went by, I saw that my father was so crushed by Teddy's death and so enraged by the events of 9/11 that he could not and would not be of much help at all. His anger boiled right beneath the surface. He walked around the house with a sullen, unapproachable expression. He did not engage with anyone and they avoided him.

My friends lined up to take baby Timmy. Everyone wanted to hold him. He was a salve to our broken hearts. Billy was sweet and charming, and people were naturally drawn to him, too. Thankfully, Jen was tucked safely in school and protected from the chaos of the days. Everyone was heartbroken for my children, so my little ones became the beautiful, tragic, therapeutic distractions to the adults in our post-9/11 world.

When Jen was home, I ran the house as normally as possible, inherently knowing how important it was to keep their structure and routine intact. No one told me to do this.

• • •

After the first week, my father left to go home to Maryland. He did not say much but I sensed he couldn't take being here any longer. My mother felt she should stay, although I know she was torn. She was very loyal to my father. They were rarely separated even for one night and I know she wanted to stay with him because they were both hurting so badly.

Instead of explaining this to me, however, she passive-aggressively repeated the details of what was involved in her reorganizing her patient load so she could stay even though she employed a woman who was able to handle it. This made me feel guilty and irritated. I understood that as the owner of a thriving occupational therapy practice leaving for four to six weeks was a big deal. Perhaps she wanted me to beg and plead for her to stay.

I recognized that it was a significant sacrifice for her to stay so long, and I did appreciate it. But she was my mother and my husband had just been killed. I *assumed* she would want to stay with me. That's what mothers do for their children in a tragedy—right? This is a perfect example of the expectations we have of the people in our family. I needed her. I needed a mother. I needed someone who would take care of me and anticipate what I needed so I could take care of everything else. My magical thinking told me she was supposed to know this and that she would want to do it.

I was well into adulthood, so, understandably, she hadn't been a mother to me in decades. She and my father had role-reversed when my mother started her practice in the late '70s. He stayed at home and did the shopping and the cooking. By September 2001, so much time had passed that it seemed my mother had lost most of her domestic skills. My mother was always more analytical than sensitive.

Throughout my life, as living examples of the perfection model of the 1950s, my parents trained me to think that they were all-knowing about all things. My magical and misinformed thinking created unrealistic expectations of them and proved to be the downfall of our relationship. Because of the family and societal instruction I had been given, I went into 9/11 believing that my parents would know what to do, would have the answers, and would be able to help me through any tragedy. But the centrifugal force of 9/11 quickly blew down that house of cards.

• • •

From a lifetime of unclear, refracted rules of communication in our family, I had never been taught or learned to ask for what I needed. Being needy was not allowed, and honest, open, two-way communication did not exist.

In the weeks that followed, my mother continued making critical and passive aggressive remarks about how I was handling things. She didn't think I should have such an open-door policy. She reminded me how much she was doing for me taking care of Timmy. It seemed she wanted to be praised and admired for doing what I assumed anyone would do in the situation. I was up to my ears in handling chaos and not in the mind-set or position to gush over someone, especially a grandmother, for doing what I considered to be a normal job.

My mother believed that you could say anything with a smile on your face, no matter how critical or judgmental. (She told me this growing up, but even as a child, it didn't seem right to me.) Dr. VK calls this the Velvet Knife. You are misled into thinking what's being said is something nice, when, in fact, it's actually cutting.

By late September, my father came up every weekend or so. But instead of helping or engaging, he would sit alone in a chair at the far side of the family room and drink. He brooded in silence, evoking a toxic cloud of misery. My mother would flit and spin around him, asking questions, trying to care for him. She hovered over him and fussed incessantly, driving both him and me crazy.

He would bark at her, as well as at the kids, for the slightest thing in the same terrifying, vicious tone I had cowered from growing up. As a spoiled, tyrannical child now in adult form, he was intolerant to anything that didn't go his way. But we didn't dare cross him. The conditioning to allow him to behave however he pleased had been instilled in me since childhood and I was still afraid to confront him. Now my children were suffering my father's bad behavior in their own house, and I was getting angry.

I wanted my parents to leave but didn't know how to ask them. I didn't have the courage or the skill set to honestly ask for what I needed. So, instead, I held my tongue and stewed in silence, with my anger and resentment building.

*   *   *

My parents are products of their generation and our culture. Neither my mother nor my father was ever introspective or self-aware. They never stood back to take stock of how the things they said were received nor how their behavior affected others. It doesn't seem that looking inward was something people did then. The superficial focus of their generation and the norms of society kept things falsely on the surface. In other words, "If it *looked* good, then it *was* good." You were expected to muscle through emotional difficulties in silence; to discuss them or admit to them was considered a shameful weakness.

It is understandable that, like my father, my mother was caught up in her own personal grief over losing Teddy. Maybe watching me go through this was too painful for her. Maybe she needed to attend to my father because she was putting herself in my place and thinking about what it would be like if she lost him. Now I understand that as much as I needed her, she was having her own experience of Teddy's death. She only had the capacity to attend to my father, he was her priority, so there was nothing left for me.

Had I understood these things about my parents when Ted died, I would not have had the expectations of them that I did.

My parents saw the situation through their own broken and refracted lenses and were awash in a vortex of grief. From where I stood, it seemed that they felt their shock was the biggest, their pain the greatest, and their loss the most complete; they were not able to see or move beyond themselves.

I was raised to be highly independent, so I was fully functioning in the weeks after Ted died. My parents were used to my competent behavior. I'm sure they assumed I was fine and didn't need them. But it still would have been nice to have a mother (or other family member) who was thinking of me and anticipating my needs, supporting me so that I could take care of my children and manage the situation I was in.

As the fall of 2001 progressed, I wanted my parents to stay in Maryland. They added work to my life and gave little benefit when they were here. Healthy boundaries did not exist for us. My parents assumed they were always welcome, but they never asked. They would announce that they were coming, and I didn't have the skills, confidence, or perceived permission to tell them "No." I didn't even know I was allowed to place a boundary around myself, so I stewed in silence.

I wish I knew then that I was allowed to set boundaries. I wish I knew then how to ask for what I needed. Perhaps I could have said to my parents as kindly and gently as possible, "I love you, but I need you to stay home. When you can be here in a supportive, positive, and helpful way, then we'd love to see you. Until then, please don't come."

CHAPTER FIVE

UNEXPECTED BEAMS OF LIGHT

The Kindness of Strangers

BRIGHT LIGHTS OF HEALING

As I continued to let people outside of our family into our lives, I was astonished by the constancy in their love and their open behavior. The kindness was beautiful. The grace was palpable. People poured out their hearts and showered us with unconditional, loving care.

As they gave to me and I received from them, I realized that we were helping each other in what I now know is a beautiful cycle of give and take. We were bonded together in this devastating, shared trauma.

My family was showered with the kindness of friends and neighbors but I was also amazed by what we received from the incredible kindness of strangers.

• • •

People loved Teddy Luckett. He had touched the hearts of many in his life. His kindness toward those he affected brought kindness to us after his death.

Hundreds of cards and letters of condolence flooded in from across the country with people's heartfelt expression of their sincerest sympathy for our family. I received beautiful messages from people who had known Ted throughout his life. Some I knew, some I had never met, but all of them expressed a deep and genuine love for the man we had lost.

As incredible as all of these messages were, the letters from the men were the most amazing: long, meaningful, often-humorous notes telling me about their friendship with Teddy and what he had meant to them. One letter described how I would see Ted reflected in my children as they grew up. This particular message stayed with me, and I have watched Ted's essence shine through each of our three children in unique ways. I often think that, between them, I almost have a complete Ted.

One day, in my need to organize the mounting mess of cards and letters and get a little control back (in my Virgo way), I threw away all the envelopes. I have always regretted doing this. There was no way I could have responded to them with all that was going on, but I have always felt badly that I did not compile a list of all those who reached out to us. If you are reading this now and you sent us something, please accept this as our very late but sincere note of gratitude.

We also received many books and pamphlets on grieving. About three weeks after 9/11, I read a passage on the back of one nondescript grief pamphlet that echoed this strange positivity I was feeling but could not quite grasp in my tangled mind.

It said, "Although we have lost so much, we still have so much left."

My heart resonated with the truth of it. I told it to Jen and Billy as I tucked them that night, and their little faces lit up with the brightest smiles. They needed to know that, one day, their sadness and confusion would subside. I wanted them to be hopeful despite our heartbreak and devastation.

*   *   *

Friends, neighbors, and people throughout the world projected themselves into our situation and I know that receiving this unexpected, unending, loving support from everyone, everywhere was the foundation of our healing.

*   *   *

The heroic and remarkable first responders, the policemen, firemen, and Port Authority officers who were lost trying to save Teddy and all the others, are revered and honored to this day. Their humanitarian efforts and personal sacrifice cannot be noted or brought to light enough; they exemplify the true essence of what it means to give selflessly; they take the concept of the *kindness of strangers* to a whole new level.

This selfless compassion of the first responders from companies around the New York Metro, was shown as they all flooded into Manhattan that morning. Rescue teams arrived from up and down the East coast and states as far as Florida, Maine, and Texas. Within hours of the attacks, these courageous and intrepid warriors organized and set out in convoys leaving their homes and their families to come and help for an undetermined amount of time; many stayed for weeks.

THE GODNESS OF 9/11

Amid the unprecedented tragedy of 9/11, an incredible beauty was revealed. It was made up of the strength and courage displayed in the struggle and the undeniable grace of the human spirit. People felt connected to one another. The unity and patriotism for our country was tangible. Compassion was everywhere. 9/11 was a great equalizer and the kindness it brought out in our collective experience was extraordinary.

I call this the Godness of 9/11 (goodness with just one "o"). It is the incredible love, support, and caring that surrounded my kids and me in the wake of 9/11. It is the magnanimous resilience of the human spirit, the kindness and care that is inherent within each of us.

In our humanness, we only imagine the negative when we think about potential trauma; the death of a spouse, a cancer diagnosis, or a sick child. But we rarely conjure up the love, the care, the support, the goodness, the *Godness* that will come with it.

In every traumatic situation, Godness always shows up because people show up. Godness arrives as the *kindness of strangers.*

. . .

The *kindness of strangers* and the fact that we continued to be remembered long after the event sustained my children and me and kept us buoyant as we healed. I believe this incredible thoughtfulness is what separates losing Ted in 9/11 versus him dying in a different way. Usually, other than close friends and family, people soon forget another's death within a matter of months. With 9/11, people have *still* not forgotten.

If we would treat each other the way my family has been treated in the aftermath of 9/11, we would live in a far kinder and gentler world. What I mean by that is, as a 9/11 family, we are always given that extra pause or moment of consideration before people judge us because they know our story. Maybe we could consider giving others that same consideration, that extra pause before we judge them, because they, too, have a significant story.

●　●　●

EVERY LITTLE BIT HELPED

In the weeks and months after 9/11, it seemed that everyone jumped in to help.

Communities rallied with foundations and fund-raising efforts to raise money for the families in their towns. Like the unity in World War II, everyone stepped up and took part in some way. Some were organized events, while others were simply collections of cash or thoughtful gifts. Children raised money with lemonade stands; youth groups, sports teams, and Scout troops came together with creative and charming efforts.

There was a tree outside of our local high school that had the name of each of the victims tied to a branch with white ribbons that looked like beautiful blossoms. A unique fund-raiser called the Children's Chain of Compassion created a paper chain that filled the football field and raised more than $20,000 for the Alliance of Neighbors of Monmouth County.

At the various fundraisers, stacks of handmade quilts and other crafts that had been sent from around the country were given to the widows and families. I received stuffed teddy bears from Texas for the kids and quilts from Connecticut. We were given beautiful artwork that expressed the artist's love and pain; we received CDs with original music written by talented singer-songwriters whose heartbreak and confusion resonated in their lyrics and melodies. We also received gifts from several large community efforts, such as Jason's Dreams for Kids and the Alliance of Neighbors.

Without my knowledge, our close friends chipped in and raised the money for Ted's Memorial Service that was held in late September of 2001; more than 1,500 people attended. They spared me having to think about this enormous event beyond the pain involved with planning the church service. This is a great example of "doing" and not "asking" in a time of crisis.

The kindness of two very important groups stands out for us personally: Cantor Fitzgerald and Ohio Wesleyan University.

Howard Lutnick, Chairman and CEO of Cantor Fitzgerald, his sister Edie Lutnick, who became the President of the Cantor Relief Fund, and his wife, Allison, created an extended family for us: the 658 families who lost a loved one who worked at Cantor Fitzgerald. Howard was not yet in the building that morning because he was taking his son to his first day of school. Within days of 9/11, the Cantor Relief Fund was formed and has been managed by Edie since its inception. The Fund distributed the promised money and health care with heartfelt and professional grace that never waivered. To this day, I still receive e-mails for Cantor Family events. Edie and Howard's younger brother Gary was killed on 9/11. Gary Lutnick was Teddy's boss at ESpeed.

A remarkable group of friends and alumni from Ohio Wesleyan University (OWU) created the Ohio Wesleyan Friends Fund to establish a scholarship in Ted's name along with another OWU friend and Cantor employee, Doug Cherry, who also died that day. They held fundraisers for ten years to build a trust fund large enough that it would generate distributions for annual scholarships in Ted's and Doug's honor each year.

OWU is a very special place, unique among thousands of colleges and universities around the country. There is a special soulfulness in the student community that creates a lifelong bond. I remember meeting Ted's OWU friends when we started dating and wishing I had gone there. They have remained my close friends and allies to this day.

In an unprecedented move, Ted's and Doug's dearest friends petitioned the school to grant academic scholarships to the six children between the Luckett and Cherry families, should they choose to attend OWU. As of this publication, five of the six kids involved have attended OWU for at least a year, with two having graduated and two still in attendance.

I believe a new charitable aspect of our world opened with 9/11. People became charity-minded. Prior to 9/11, I don't remember corporate America making it a priority to actively engage with charitable entities. Within months of 9/11, every company, both large and small, created or became affiliated with a meaningful 501(c)(3) foundation. It is now second nature that organizations, social groups, and families have charities that they support.

As extreme and negative as 9/11 was, this beauty and thoughtfulness, the caring for each other that came pouring forth, is unprecedented by any other experience in my life. Columbine, Oklahoma City, and 9/11 set a precedent for the many collective traumas that we have experienced since, and the Godness is present each time. People show up for each other. People care. We just need to see them in the light between the cracks.

• • •

THAT FIRST CHRISTMAS

When the holidays came in 2001, the *kindness of strangers* appeared in force. Again, cards and letters flooded in from across the country with beautiful, heartfelt messages.

Our dear local friends and first responders in Fair Haven made our Christmas and New Year's after 9/11 truly special.

On Christmas Eve 2001, a fire truck pulled up in front of our house with lights and sirens blaring. We opened the door to see many volunteer firemen (all of whom I knew), walk up our driveway with armfuls of presents for Jen, Billy, and Timmy. I'm sure they did the same thing for the other two families in town who had young children who had lost their father on 9/11.

I personally received an unexpected collection of beautiful anonymous presents from my girlfriends and the women in my community—the sacred feminine at its best. That first Christmas season was such a painful and lonely time, I was so grateful for their love and kindness. But there were no cards on the gifts, so I never knew whom to thank. So if you're reading this now, and you were part of giving us that special Christmas, thank you from the bottom of my heart. Your thoughtfulness and consideration lifted me up at a tragically low point in my life.

This was the "years of firsts" and it was our first Christmas without Teddy. The pressure of the holidays from the outside world was enormous and intensified the stress and negativity that had been building between my parents and me. Although we went into Christmas as well as could be expected, by New Year's Eve relations with the adults in my family hit an all-time low.

Our hearts ached from the gigantic hole left in our lives from losing Teddy. The holidays brought out his absence in an even more glaring way. By Christmas afternoon, the letdown set in, and our house became sadder with each passing hour. After a long, emotional holiday season with too many days of people in my house, too little space, stuff piled in every corner, and a workload I cannot describe, I was starting to come out of my skin. I needed it to be over.

But the morning after Christmas, my mother came down with the flu. The following night, Billy got the stomach bug and a fever. I was terrified that these sicknesses would make the rounds through everyone. I needed my father to take my mother home. Meanwhile, all I could do was sanitize every surface in the house and try not to lose my mind.

For two days, I begged my brother and father to take my mother home, but they wouldn't. I know she was sick, but they could have bundled her up for the car ride to Maryland. They did not seem to understand that I could not afford to get sick as a single mother of three very young children. They did not understand that if I became ill, there was no one to back me up.

I had suspected my parents wanted to stay to meet my brother's new girlfriend, who was coming from Seattle to celebrate New Year's with my brother in New York. That turned out to be the case and when they finally did all leave by midday on December 31, I was relieved beyond belief.

My house was a disorganized mess, with stuff piled everywhere, laundry from sickness on top of the regular loads, and food and clutter packed into every spare inch.

I was barely hanging on having almost reached my breaking point. I continued to feel the reverberation of the incredible emotional stress I'd been under even though my family was finally gone. When I looked at the mountain of work before me I wanted to scream.

I did what I could to manage the mess, then sat down with my kids to cuddle together by ourselves in our quiet house and watch a movie. I gave them an early dinner, a peaceful bath, and put them to bed.

Around eight o'clock, I went downstairs to chill by myself for the first time in weeks. I was clicking through the channels when I felt the familiar ache of a fever coming on. *Of course.* Now, what was I going to do? What I had feared most was happening, and there was no one to help me. It was then that I let go. I sat there racked with sobs, unable to catch my breath. I don't think I could have felt more bereft or despondent.

The doorbell rang sometime later, startling me out of my demoralized state of self-pity. When I opened the door, no one was there. A plain white envelope was taped at eye level. When I looked inside I saw that it was filled with cash and a note wrapped around it said:

Dear Lisa,

Happy New Year!
Please don't ever consider moving.
We love you, and we hope you will stay.

Love,
Your Neighbors

Once again, saved by the thoughtful, unexpected grace of the *kindness of strangers.*

. . .

As time passed, I continued to have to make a conscious effort to allow myself to receive. I knew it was necessary for all of us, but sometimes it wasn't easy.

Our town is small, and everyone knew me. When I went out for groceries, I would anticipate encountering others and the awkward moments that would follow. I could feel their sadness, pain, and their fear of not knowing what to say. As uncomfortable as it might have felt at times, receiving love and support was helping me, and I was afraid that, if I closed myself off to it, it would stop.

Without knowing it then, I had created a practice to allow myself to be helped and, at the same time, help others. Was it possible that I was growing and expanding through this tragedy? Through all of this had I begun to realize that embracing humility and gratitude made me a better person, that a strong, loving force was guiding me, and that the healing power of love and prayer is real?

Even though my heart was broken over the loss of Teddy, it was overflowing with love because of the phenomenon called the *kindness of strangers*, and I became determined to bear witness to this miracle.

CHAPTER SIX

RIDING OUT THE STORM

How I Made It Through

LIFE PREPARED ME FOR LIFE

By being prepared for Ted's death, I didn't have to manage the shock of 9/11 in the same way as everyone else. If I had not had this macabre planning, my experience would have been very different and significantly more difficult. But because of this bizarre preparation, I found myself standing firmly in an offensive position from a well-thought out, objective place.

THE ROAD MAP OF HOW NOT TO DO IT

By the time I reached adulthood, I was terrified at the thought of someone I loved dying.

My father's tragic story of his parents' early deaths, and the subsequent damage and misery that followed, was dark and foreboding. Having witnessed his unhappy life, I was afraid of the pain I imagined that would come with death. My father spoke of his experiences only on rare occasions, but I watched his behavior and felt his pain every day. My father's losses were my only truth of how death was handled and experienced.

I didn't realize it at the time but I had a second example of how grief was refracted and mishandled, and the ongoing, endless misery that followed, when a close friend's father died when we were in junior high school.

Debbie and I had been friends since the third grade. She was the only one who stuck with me in middle school, despite my becoming a social pariah. Debbie was tough and independent and didn't care what anyone thought. Although moody and irritable by nature, she had a unique charm, and I loved her. I know I often annoyed her, but I also know that she loved me, too.

We spent our preteen years swimming like mermaids and watching *The Brady Bunch* and *The Partridge Family* during Friday night sleepovers. I was so grateful for her friendship. As we got older, I felt lucky to have anyone who would talk to me, let alone hang out with me.

Over the years, I got to know Debbie's family well. Debbie's mother, Sue, was a nice woman who started teaching us to bake and sew when we met at age nine. This was the beginning of my life as a crafter. Debbie and I loved crafting. We spent hours together during our friendship learning everything from knitting to basket weaving to learning to throw pottery on a wheel.

Sue loved to talk and I listened with polite interest. She would tell me about her life and her sad and broken childhood. Sue had been sent away to boarding school as a young girl when she was still in elementary school. She talked about how lonely she had been and how unloved she had felt by both of her parents. Even as a young girl, I could feel her pain and insecurity, probably because I had so much of my own.

Looking back, I remember feeling honored and important that a grown-up would take me into her confidence. I thought I was special because she would ask me a million questions about my life. Eventually though, I realized that she never listened to my answers–she just asked question after question. As I got older, I watched her do the same thing with other people. Years later in analysis, I learned that her behavior was really anxiety and insecurity fueled by a desperate need for attention.

Debbie's father died of a heart attack when we were in eighth grade, and I watched their family come unglued in the wake of his death. He was the first person I knew who died; I projected myself into their situation and was heartbroken for them. The community came out in droves to support them, and they were showered with love, support, and attention. He was a well-known and respected leader in the community, so his death was a significant loss for everyone.

However, as the years went by, it seemed that no one in Debbie's family could move past it. Maybe they felt they would be dishonoring their father's memory or in some way disrespecting him if they did. Sue set the tragic tone for her children and talked about him incessantly. A few of their close family friends also could not move on, which further enabled their behavior.

In our college years when I would see Sue, Debbie, and her siblings, they still talked about their father constantly; not in the lighthearted way that many people share fond memories of a lost loved one but sadly and dramatically as though he had died only recently.

Conversations were always somehow redirected toward his death. They acted as though they were the only ones who had ever lost someone. I got the sense that they felt they were never allowed to be happy again.

Something was wrong with this picture, but who was I to judge? I put myself in their place and felt great sympathy for them. I still had both of my parents so I couldn't possibly know what they were going through. The only way I could even imagine their pain was by relating their experience back to my father's losses.

But now I know that they were subconsciously stuck in a victim mentality. They were defining themselves by their loss, and they were awash in the attention their father's death brought them. Sue's emotional damage from her childhood played out in her leadership of the family. Their father's death gave them a brief celebrity status, and they were finally being seen. The feelings of being special and getting so much attention was too intoxicating to release. I think that, in their minds, if they were to heal, then people would forget about them and move on. Because Sue had been so deprived, she role-modeled for her children that negative attention was still better than no attention at all, so they continued to play the role of victims.

As time passed, it became so depressing (and annoying) to be around them that I stayed away. As we entered adulthood, Debbie and I grew apart, but the experience of watching her family suffer never again finding joy after their father's death, always stayed with me.

I discussed Debbie's family with Dr. VK and learned about the nuances of victimization so I could avoid taking my children down this negative, life-wasting path.

Because of my father's and Debbie's family's examples, when I would think about Ted's death during those sleepless nights in the years before he died, I could only imagine tidal waves of excruciating pain, horrible, dark sadness, and endless suffering. I thought that if someone I loved ever died, my life would be ruined and I would never be happy again. Witnessing these death experiences made me absolutely terrified of my own future losses.

But when Teddy did actually die, my experience could not have been more opposite. By being prepared in these strange ways, the insights I received in the first weeks after 9/11 were simply remarkable. My expectations had been completely one-sided because I had never known about the Godness that would come with the experience. Living with my father's unprocessed grief and anger, along with witnessing Debbie's family live as victims, defined by their loss, gave me a unique "road map of how not to do it."

So in the weeks after 9/11, my plan was simple: I would take my kids in the opposite direction.

HOW I GRIEVED

After the initial, dramatic intensity of the first moments that fateful morning, I became numb. I had my hands full with my babies, friends, neighbors, family, and the enormous calamity that engulfed us all. Through the first year, I couldn't even get to Teddy. The reality of his death just wouldn't stick. My logical mind tried to come to grips with it, but my heart wouldn't let it sink in.

My initial grief came in waves—first, for my kids. How could he not be there for them? What would their lives be like without their father? How was it possible that they would never know their wonderful dad? Driving the kids to school in the mornings in those first weeks, I would see men walking with their kids and get angry. Having irrational rants with myself, I'd think, *How come that guy's alive and Ted isn't? What about my kids? OMG! This is so unfair!* I couldn't believe he was gone.

The next thing I grieved was what Ted had lost: that he would never see his children grow up. This was completely unexpected, based on the examples of my father and Debbie's family. The grief I had witnessed with them was focused on the people who were left, not the one that was gone, but, surprisingly, I was incredibly sad for Ted.

Waves of my own grief would wash over me. As intense as they were, in a strange way, I was glad to feel them. The pain connected me to Teddy. I would be standing in my closet or making my bed and suddenly be overcome by a powerful longing, a deep heartache, and a flood of tears. Nighttime was the hardest, of course, but, during the day, the rush wouldn't last long. I was so busy that something would distract me, and I'd snap back out of it. Somehow I knew to let Nature take its course, allowing it to flow naturally, and to gratefully take the breaks that were given to me.

The tidal wave of crushing pain that I had expected to feel when I imagined Ted's death never came and that acute, constant pain that I thought would be with me for the rest of my life never materialized. The pain came in waves that ebbed and flowed. It was acute and intense at first, but it lessened as the years went by. It was so much different than I had expected; incredibly I had actually made it worse in my imagination.

I missed Teddy terribly, but initially my grief was more about the confusion of what life now looked like. It was worry for my children's loss and the anticipation of their futures; their pain was my pain times three. My grief was the void left from losing my life partner and the shared memory of our history together. It was the phone ringing that was never Teddy calling—I so missed hearing his voice. It was his complete absence in my life: getting up in the morning, sitting next to me in the car, walking in after work, eating at the dinner table with the kids, and holding each other at night in bed.

I did my best to stay in the day. I was in this new place of self-trust, and so distracted by the chaos around me that I allowed myself to feel whatever came next and tried not to overanalyze my thoughts. I would ride the wave of happy, sad, angry, normal, frustrated, numb, or busy as hell, but I never did get that constant, overwhelming pain I had imagined that would leave me incapacitated forever.

My beautiful little kids were pure joy, innocence, and love. They needed to have a normal, happy life, and I was determined to get us there. So we stayed in the moment, moved through our daily routine, and rolled with things as they came and went.

The kids balanced the sadness in our household with their natural childhood effervescence. They couldn't comprehend the finality of death or that Ted was gone forever. They were protected in their own little bubbles. As long as they felt safe in that moment, they were okay.

When they got older and went through puberty, the reality of their father's death became real. All three of my kids cycled through their grief at different times; they were not spared the pain. I have learned there is no avoiding grief; it is something we all must go through. When children are young, grief may be delayed, but it is always there, waiting in the wings.

Before Teddy's death, I had no formal understanding of grief beyond what I had witnessed in my childhood. Like most people, I had heard of the five stages of grief: denial, anger, bargaining, depression, and acceptance, propounded by Elisabeth Kubler Ross in 1969. Interestingly, I didn't hear much about this in the years after 9/11, but I also didn't attend any support groups, where I'm sure it was discussed.

I was given many books on grief, but the only one I read cover to cover was called *Guiding Your Child Through Grief* by James and Mary Ann Emswiler. The most important concept, which we enacted immediately, was to set up a "holding community" for Jennifer in her elementary school with the principal, school nurse, social worker, art teacher, and her homeroom teacher.

If Jen needed to leave class, she was allowed to go see whomever she chose, but after a little chat and a hug, she would gently be sent back to class. These women protected Jennifer by giving her genuine love and care and much needed structure to make her feel safe. Jen and I credit them with getting her through that first year after her daddy's death as well as could ever be expected. Jen never missed a day of school. I sent her every day because I felt it was the safest place for her to be, away from the television and the panicky buzz in the adult world. Jen did not see the news footage of the buildings burning and falling until she was in high school.

I broke the news to my children over several days. First I said there had been a fire and no one had been heard from yet, but that Ted was probably okay. Then I said many people were missing, and we couldn't find him. Finally, I said that he had died in the fire. Two years later, when Billy was in first grade, he experienced his first fire drill. Needless to say, he flipped out. I never made the connection or thought to prepare him for this inevitable school event. From then on, I asked the school to let me know when a fire drill was planned so I could warn Billy or pick him up from school to miss it.

Anyone who has been through horrible trauma or tragedy knows there are moments of normalcy that come with it, too. They may be subtle and spread apart, but they are there. I would laugh amid my pain, finding humor in a funny moment. I felt the warmth of camaraderie and fellowship with the people around me. Sometimes I felt like I was being held in suspended animation, like nothing had really happened. Other times, I felt completely alone, even in a room full of people. But with time, these waves lessened considerably.

TRUSTING MYSELF

My life shifted completely on the morning of 9/11 when I started listening to and believing in myself. I learned to stand independently as a warrior and trusted what I knew to be true. It wasn't easy to step away from what I had been taught, but I saw a new light. The limited beliefs I had been raised with in my family and in society were based in fear, shame, and punishment, and were enforced by judgment and criticism if I did not conform. I could no longer worry about them.

I began to separate myself from people whose fearful thinking and judgmental behavior made me doubt myself and threatened to pull me off my path.

With the experience of 9/11, I could see that the old, long-established thinking of past generations no longer contained the answers. A lifetime of insecurity, of trying to fit in and please everyone, was over. Maybe I was alone in this new thinking, but it was better than feeling the uncertainty of self-doubt. I had been a maverick all my life, but had never fully acted on it; now out of the box, I trusted that I was finally in the right place.

There are no coincidences. Looking back on my life, it is clear to me that I was given this difficult path to travel so I would learn as I have. Now with my continued daily practice of listening to myself, I trust that my intuition is showing me an incredible and positive future.

HEALTHY DISTRACTION THROUGH GRIEF

Lastly, it is okay, even important, to have healthy distraction while you grieve. I don't mean numbing, medicating, or avoiding the pain, but rather giving grief the respect it deserves and allowing it the time and space it needs to wash over you naturally.

At first, the shock and pain seem so acute that you can't imagine you'll ever come through the dark night of the soul.

But you will. You will be angry and sad and lost for a while trying to understand why this happened to you. But if you don't get stuck in victimhood or make it worse by judging yourself through the process, you will get through it and be okay. There is no timing other than your own. Trust that your grief will shift and morph often throughout your lifetime but you will never lose the connection to the person you loved.

Healthy distraction while you're going through grief will help you to offset the time and allow your mind to process the experience. Being in nature can be very beneficial and soothing. Any creative outlet you are compelled toward should be tried. I recommend working with your hands and fingertips because your sense of touch naturally calms your central nervous system. Tapping into sensory input, from any of your five senses, will help you to feel better; trust your sixth sense (intuition) to guide you through it.

VOICES OF INSPIRATION

The business I started with Rick K became an amazing and beneficial, healthy distraction after Ted's death helping me to get through the first year after 9/11 in an inspired and remarkable way.

Rick and I collaborated through the winter of 2002 to find a project that we agreed on. His idea was a documentary called *The Aftermath of 9/11*. It was very dark and sad, focusing on the destruction and loss. But I didn't want to be involved with anything negative.

Instead, because I was experiencing such mind-blowing beauty and positivity, the negative actually seemed small by comparison—or maybe I just couldn't hold onto it. Of course, I understood the horror of the experience, but, to me, 9/11 was how Ted died. It was his heart attack, car accident, or cancer. I couldn't stop seeing how people rallied around us, were supporting us unconditionally, and weren't forgetting about us.

I understood people's rage and fear over this unprecedented act of terrorism, but I had processed my anger over terrorism after the first bombing in 1993. I know it's strange that after 9/11, I didn't get angry again. Maybe that's because in the recesses of my mind I knew Ted had chosen to go back into an enormous target. Maybe because my mind wasn't filled with the fury and hatred of this latest outrageous act, there was room instead for me to comprehend the beauty and graciousness of the human spirit that followed.

I was now immersed in a very different experience. I could not seem to focus on the negative. Yes I had tragically lost my husband and the father of my children, but raising them and living our busy lives together each day was saving me. We were getting through it. The loving energy that was being showered on us from friends and strangers around the world kept us buoyant. Every day, I saw signs from Ted and the Other Side that kept me light and hopeful. If I stayed in the day, life was okay, even good.

A story Rick told me about Carl Perkins kept echoing in my mind. Carl had suffered tragic losses in his lifetime and had many disappointments in his career, but he never gave up. One day, Rick asked him how it was he was able to keep going, time after time. He answered simply, "It's my music. My music got me through." Music was Carl Perkins's "Voice" for healing.

Voices of Inspiration was an idea Rick had for a radio or television show that Carl Perkins would host, interviewing other musicians telling their stories of healing through music. Carl didn't live long enough to see it through to fruition, but I wanted *Voices of Inspiration*. I loved the idea. But to me *Voices of Inspiration* wasn't just about music; it meant any type of "voice" as a metaphor for a creative outlet someone used to heal.

In the winter of 2002, we met Bar Scott, a singer-songwriter from Woodstock, New York. One of the many things I learned from Rick is that the world is filled with talented people. Bar Scott is one of them. Bar's original soulful sound spoke to me. Her music was sad and beautiful. My kids loved it, too. We listened to it in the years that followed Ted's death, and it helped us process our grief and soothed us as we healed.

Rick reached out to Bar in the winter of 2002 only to learn that she had just nine weeks before lost her three-and-a-half-year-old son and only child, Forrest, to a rare liver cancer. Although I was so sad about Teddy, it was inconceivable to me to lose a child.

Rick went to meet Bar and her husband, Peter, the following week. He filmed Bar sitting at the piano, playing and singing her music, telling the details of her story. She was raw and open, honest and beautiful. Her pain was palpable and pure. Bar Scott was the living personification of *Voices of Inspiration*.

. . .

In early May 2002, it was announced that Ground Zero would close on May 30, 2002. I had not yet been to New York to see it, but I knew I needed to go.

Lt. Commander William Keegan had worked for the Port Authority (PA) for twenty-eight years. Keegan was honored to run the night shift at the site for the nine-month duration of the cleanup effort. It is thought that he logged in the highest number of hours of anyone who worked at Ground Zero.

Lt. Commander Keegan oversaw and helped manage the seventeen trade unions that worked around the clock. Normally, this could be a volatile combination of personalities; but these men worked together, side by side, without incident, for those nine months. They were doing God's work. It was their honor to do it. They worked boldly, trying to exorcise the terroristic poison and the pain of their own losses, finishing what should have taken two years in a record nine months.

People come into our lives for a reason. For me, Bill Keegan was one of them. Bill speaks like a poet laureate—his descriptions and choice of words, his philosophy and worldview is extraordinary. Bill Keegan is a very special man.

Rick had been trying to meet with Bill Keegan for months. By May 2002, Bill had rejected Rick's many requests for an interview. Too many people were trying to get his story. He wisely wasn't buying into the media circus. So, as a last resort, Rick asked me to try.

Somewhat shamefully, I called Bill a few days before the site was due to close. It was a Saturday night, and as I dialed I remember thinking, *Here I am, alone again. God, is this really my future?* It was a sad and lonely time that, in that moment, I thought might last forever.

Bill answered his phone, and I told him who I was. I said that I had not yet been to Ground Zero but wanted to see it before it closed. I told him I was working with a television producer and asked if it would be okay if we came in to film his last "roll call" with his men before they started the final night shift as the site was closing the next day. I was uncomfortable using my position in this way, but something told me it was important. I think he agreed only because I was a widow.

At 6:00 PM on May 29, Rick and I, and one cameraman, went to Ground Zero to meet with Lt. Commander Bill Keegan and his men.

When we arrived, I was disoriented by the lower Manhattan that I found. What felt like dozens of city blocks had been leveled and excavated. The sixteen-acre, seventy-foot deep gaping hole where World Trade Center Towers and surrounding buildings had been was enormous. The only thing I recognized, having lived and worked in New York City for so many years, was the Century 21 department store sign that had once been blocks away from Ted's office. Now everything was in the wrong place. It was completely surreal.

The Port Authority (PA) manages the airports, bridges, tunnels, and mass transit servicing New York and New Jersey. It is funded by both states and comanaged by the governors. Since the World Trade Center was owned and managed by the PA, they had jurisdiction over the cleanup of the site. The PA office was a double-wide trailer that sat adjacent to the fencing on the North side of Ground Zero.

Once inside the PA trailer, I found an office in the front, a large room with chairs and desks in the center, and a U-shaped area in the back. The U-shaped area was the PA's personal memorial tribute with photos and artwork for their thirty-seven men and women who were lost when the buildings fell. It was then that I saw, for the first time, the famous painting of an angel looking down and reaching out to take the hand of a woman in a business suit who is reaching up from a window of one of The Towers.

Rick, the cameraman, and I were standing on one side, toward the front of the room.

Lt. Commander Keegan began his roll call. He spoke for twenty minutes to the seventy or so men dressed in dusty overalls, sitting in chairs, and lining the walls of the room. He talked about the honor and diligence of their mission. He discussed the details of the next day's ceremony, when the commemorative, last steel beam would be taken from Ground Zero and who would walk beside it. He discussed how they had been away from their families and would be returning to them for the first time in months. The energy in the room was serious and sad. I could feel the intensity of their exhaustion, pain, and emotion.

It was then that I was hit with two revelations:

First: These were the men who had been looking for Teddy every day . . . with their hands. These men were spending twelve-hour shifts literally sifting through the dirt on the floor of Ground Zero, picking up anything that was larger than a quarter, in search of bone fragments. They had sorted and sifted through hundreds of feet of debris and human remains for months until they were left with only dirt. What they had seen had been horrible. What they found in the wreckage was indescribable. But they stoically did their job with patriotic pride, honor, and a sense of purpose. They left nothing untouched. I knew in that moment I was seeing something no one yet knew about and that it was very, very important.

Second: These men were about to hit an emotional wall they'd been distracted from for months. The next day, they would be going back to the jobs and lives they had been living before 9/11, but now as very different men. They had gone to war. They were devastated. The silence would be deafening. They had sacrificed so much, but the work that had kept them going was now finished. They now had thoughts and memories from which they could not escape. Theirs was a unique grief. Intuitively, I knew they were in trouble, and I was very worried for them.

When Lt. Commander Keegan finished speaking, he asked for questions. No one said anything. I was faced with one of those moments when you know that if you don't say something, you'll regret it for the rest of your life. So with my stomach in knots, I took a deep breath and raised a shaky hand. In a quavering, tearful voice, thick with emotion and gratitude, a voice that made everyone in the room squirm in their seats, I thanked those men, from the bottom of my heart, and promised to tell everyone I knew what they had been doing for me—for us—the families of the victims of 9/11.

Going home on the ferry that night, I told Rick we needed to do something for them. They needed to be recognized and honored for their heroic efforts. We needed to thank them publicly. We needed to tell the world what we had seen. We needed to do a *Voices of Inspiration* concert for them—to rally them, acknowledge them, support them, and show them how much we cared and how much we appreciated what they had done. Now I understood what I'd been working toward those past eight months and I felt the solid truth of it.

I was compelled to do this from somewhere deep within, driven by an intense pull that was powerful, positive, and all consuming. I profoundly understood what their families had also sacrificed on our behalves. They were my heroes, and I felt an urgent need to let them know that I "saw" them, that I understood, and how much I cared.

My friend Tom Thees and I produced the show. We booked the 2,900-seat Beacon Theater in New York City for July 22, 2002, and hired Rick as director. We had six weeks to put together *Voices of Inspiration—A Universal Hug.*

Bill Keegan put the word out and invited his men and their families along with the men from the other seventeen trade unions who had worked so closely together.

We headlined the concert with singers Phoebe Snow, Beth Neilson Chapman, and Bar Scott, women who had all suffered terrible traumas in their lives and had healed themselves by expressing their pain through their music. Garry Tallant, the bassist for Bruce Springsteen, was the music director; Bobby Bandiero, who also played with the E-Street Band, played guitar. Former Springsteen vocalists Delores and Layonne Holmes and several other female singers sang back up.

As the host of the show, I made the transitions between acts by telling my part of the story. I felt very comfortable on stage; I was in the flow of something far greater than me and could have stayed there forever. Jen and Billy were in the audience. My beautiful Jen, who was then eight years old, got the message loud and clear. She still talks about how proud she felt watching me in that moment, on the stage of the famous Beacon Theater in New York, sharing the love.

When the musical portion concluded, Bill Keegan came up and addressed the audience. In his remarkable eloquence, Bill shared his profound philosophies from his experience of 9/11. He introduced men and women from all of the seventeen unions, the volunteers, and the clergy, many of whom Rick had filmed. One by one, they came up on stage, and Bill spoke personally about their commitment, courage, and fortitude. It was their moment. Through their pain I could see their radiance; they were shining.

When the show was ending, Bill unexpectedly called me back out onstage. I was presented with three crosses as gifts of thanks: one from the Port Authority cut from the white marble from the North Tower lobby, and two from the Iron Workers' Local 40, cut from recovered steel from the North Tower.

The crosses are incredibly special, and I am honored to have them. The white, marble cross is slightly larger than the two six-inch steel crosses. I had them framed in beautiful shadow boxes, and they are centered high on a shelf that is our little altar to 9/11. I am so grateful that, one day, Jen, Billy, and Timmy will each have a cross of their own from this very special time.

The Voices of Inspiration: A Universal Hug concert was a success. We now had original film of the concert, valuable interviews, original music by talented artists, and a unique story of the 9/11 experiences. The next logical step was to put it together, so Rick went to work to edit and produce an hour-long, televised docu-concert.

The docu-concert's title became: *Voices of Inspiration—A Universal Hug: A Thank You Concert for the 9/11 Rescue and Recovery Workers.*

Rick interviewed rescue and recovery workers, volunteers, and clergy from the floor of Ground Zero. They were open and candid about their experiences. Many of these strong men cried openly. One night, Bar Scott and several other female vocalists met Rick and Bill Keegan at Ground Zero, where they sang prayers and communed their grace from that sacred space amid the presence of thousands of lost souls. It was a remarkable moment in time that summer; the human connection and spirituality was strong and beautiful. Everyone felt the power of it. The "Force" was with us all.

For several weeks after the concert, Rick combined these interviews from Ground Zero with the music and stories by Phoebe, Beth, and Bar, set to my voice-overs. There was footage of Bill and me walking through Ground Zero the night before the site closed. There was footage of the late, great Delores Holmes opening the show singing "Dig All Night." There was footage of Bill calling everyone up onstage. There was footage of me crying as I spoke at the Last Roll Call. *Voices of Inspiration—A Thank You Concert* told the story of the rescue and recovery workers and what we had seen. We had done it. Now it was time to share it with the world.

During that first year, my family thought I should be staying home and attending to daily life as a new widow with now-fatherless children. But I couldn't sit still. A higher power was driving me; too much was happening. People thought I was crazy to be running a business and producing concerts. But I had so much energy I was able to do it. And I did it well. I did not neglect my children. Not only were they well cared for by me, but they were also given balance and stability with our new family, the Embry-Doubtfires. My kids were shown that, even in the saddest tragedies, there are beautiful silver linings to be found. It was a surreal and extraordinary time.

We shopped the one-hour show to several of the New York television stations with Channel 9, WWOR-TV, choosing to air it as their highlight tribute to the first-year anniversary of 9/11. It aired twice on September 11, 2002. The station titled their media effort *A New Day Dawning.* The positive philosophy from the station's management was perfectly aligned with how I saw things.

As August came to a close, and the first anniversary of 9/11 drew near, I was ready to stop. It had been a manic and remarkable year on immeasurable levels. Now it was time to be quiet and still. I needed to regroup, collect my little kids, and just be us again. I had done my best; I had learned a ton. I had gotten through the "year of firsts." I needed to settle down, pull in, and just "be."

The projects with Rick saved me from tipping into the abyss. It was an incredible gift of meaningful, productive distraction that filled my mind and fed my soul, and I know Ted was with me all the way. If I hadn't done it, I would have lost my mind. The negative didn't seem to stick; I could not help but be drawn to the positive. To this day, I cannot help but to effortlessly find the positive in almost any situation. I had been given the gift of the Godness of 9/11 and gratefully lived it to its fullest extent.

On September 11, 2002, Rick and I watched our television docu-concert, sitting in the Green Room at WWOR-TV Channel 9 Studios in Secaucus, New Jersey at 8:00 PM.

That night, I drove home by myself. And the first year was over.

CHAPTER SEVEN

A GLIMMER OF SELF-LOVE

The Road Back Home to Myself

In addition to my family issues and the social struggles I had, the third source of my self-loathing came from academics. I received Bs and Cs and a couple of Ds in high school, regardless of how hard I tried. When I brought home a less-than-stellar report card (which was most of them), my mother would remind me that she had received straight As in school. I think she figured that, by telling me how well she had done, her success would transfer to me through osmosis.

When I got a bad grade, I looked at it, shamed myself for being such a failure, and moved on. There were no other consequences or follow-up. I didn't know how to advocate for myself or to go in for extra help. I don't remember this being suggested by either the teachers or my parents. I guess you could say I slipped through the cracks.

It was the early '70s, and things were so crazy in our culture that, like my confused mind, the educational system was all over the place. I remember we had open classrooms with four classes being taught simultaneously, separated only by partial dividers. Students' schedules were made up of twenty-minute mods (an appropriate term in the '70s) with classes being either two or three mods—forty or sixty minutes long.

When you had a free mod, you could go wherever you wanted. Leaving campus was easy then, because, in 1971, the legal voting age was lowered to eigtheen, so some seniors could sign themselves out of school as adults. In fact, with little risk, anyone could sneak out of school in the middle of the day, regardless of their grade. Kids smoked cigarettes on the steps outside of the senior wing and could walk across the street to smoke pot on the public playground. There were kids who left school to drink at the local bars during the day. Life in the 1970s felt like a loose and unbridled free-for-all.

Looking back, my education seems marginal, and I was from one of the best school districts in the state. I don't remember much emphasis being put on study skills nor on any type of emotional education. I was not a natural student so school was always hard for me. Because of my undiagnosed learning disabilities, when I wasn't lost, I was bored. I was so twisted up emotionally that, even on a good day, school was an uphill battle. I was also constantly distracted by that nasty voice in my head telling me how much I hated myself and what a loser I was.

By high school I realized that neither my parents nor my teachers were going to help me so I was left, lost and struggling, to fend for myself. However, I am very grateful that my parents let my marginal grades slide. I was already in a serious state of depression and deep self-hatred; I had begun to think of suicide often. If they had added more negative pressure to get good grades on top of everything else I was living with, it would probably have pushed me over the edge.

•   •   •

One day when I was in my twenties my mother mentioned, in passing, that my IQ score had come back so high that they retested me. She joked that they had thought there was "gum stuck in the machine." The second round of testing came back high, but not as high as the first score.

I never thought much about it, but years later, when I was telling Dr. VK the story, she stopped short.

"Wait a minute," she said. "They retested you for your IQ?"

"Yes," I replied. "Can't you have good and bad testing days?"

"It doesn't work like that. IQ is the hard drive of your mind. There's no way to change it," she answered.

When I asked her about the second test being lower, she said, "With your low self-esteem and the unspoken household messages, you diluted the first performance."

I thought about that for a minute and said, "Well then, if I'm so smart, why didn't I do better in school?"

She replied, "IQ can be unactualized by childhood anxiety and attention issues."

My father had a high IQ and a fantastic, visionary mind; he could process concepts quickly and read extremely fast. Later I learned that, despite his high intelligence, my father, too, had not done well in high school. This is probably why he didn't give me too much heat for my grades. I came to realize that he, too, may have had learning disabilities or that the death of his father when he was fourteen derailed him so much that he lost his footing and focus.

Of course, it doesn't matter how high my IQ is, but it does explain why I can remember random, detailed facts and specifics, have multidimensional visionary ideas, and process certain things very quickly, despite having been a marginal student.

* * *

Why am I telling you this story? Because people with certain kinds of high intelligence can be regarded as a little kooky or socially awkward and while they may not do well in school it doesn't change their brilliance.

By the time I was in my early forties, I had spent my lifetime thinking I was stupid and inferior to everyone. Only recently have I accepted the truth of my kind of intelligence. It is amazing how long it has taken me to unwrite so many years of misunderstanding. It's also amazing how many different types of intelligence there are.

How our intelligence unfolds is influenced by factors such as levels of sensitivity, natural compassion, foundational security or insecurity, aggressive or passive natures, life experiences, and family circumstances. This means that we each receive information, process the experience, and handle the same event in our own unique way.

Intelligence shows in many ways. Today we value academics as the primary way to measure it. I believe that, in the future, new variations of "intelligence," like autism, will take us to incredible new places.

BLOWN OUT OF THE PROVERBIAL BOX

When the buildings fell on the morning of 9/11, I was blown out of that horrible, constrictive, narrow box that I had been struggling to fit in to. I see now that 9/11 set me free.

I needed to figure things out and fast. Not only did I need to function sanely in the daily chaos, but I also needed to protect and guide my kids through this turmoil, while keeping them as unscathed as humanly possible.

With my newly found self-trust, I followed my instincts, asked for help from Dr. VK, and set off on the most remarkable interior expedition of my life.

I went into therapy with awareness of the shame and judgment that surrounded it. It was no surprise that my parents were unsupportive. The few friends I told mumbled awkwardly, "Oh, really?" Some even scoffed at the idea.

God! Everyone was so worried about what other people would think. But for the first time in my life, I did not care at all. I did not have the luxury of caring. I knew people were wrong in their judgments and that their reactions were coming from a place of fear.

But I was now living in a different dimension and beginning to see light between the cracks. Although it would have been nice to have support, I did not need anyone's approval. Getting help for my children and me was so much more important than avoiding a little social stigma.

The physical fitness boom of the 70s and 80s led to better overall awareness about the importance of physical health today. With all the loss, heartache, and fear that has come from the natural disasters and man-made events over the past seventeen years, isn't it time for us to focus on our emotional wellness? We can also learn the skill sets needed to live happier, more emotionally educated lives filled with satisfaction, balance, empathy, compassion, and self-love. We just have to decide to make it a priority.

Contrary to popular opinion, going to therapy is not for the weak. It takes enormous courage to show up and do the work. To all those seeking a life of better understanding and emotional freedom, remember how brave you are, and go for it!

With regard to our emotional future, my favorite mottos are: "Choose Courage" and "Stigma Is Stupid!"

CHAPTER EIGHT

A POINT OF LIGHT
IN THE DISTANCE

Correcting My Refracted Lens

9/11 gave me the opportunity to reach for emotional wellness. Because I had had such a good experience in therapy when Ted and I were first married, I knew how important it would be to go after 9/11. As all my "emotional bones" were now broken, going to the doctor for my mind was the most important thing I could do for my children and me.

So I began digging through my life. I went to Dr. VK twice a week in the first six months because things were so intense and confusing on every front: children, society, family, friends, strangers, and the event of 9/11 itself. From our very first hour together, I gained useful knowledge.

Dr. VK told me, "Your life experience provides grist for the therapy mill." This has echoed in my mind for years—that you grind up emotional grain to become the flour of insight.

She never said much in sessions, and, initially, I found this to be a little disconcerting. Unlike sitting across from Laura S in a conversational setting, I would lie on a couch facing the wall with Dr. VK sitting behind me, listening quietly and taking notes.

It turns out that the reason for this is that when we face each other, we make eye contact. We watch the response from the other person and subconsciously (or consciously) alter our story. Since it is within the nuances of the report that the insights are hidden, the least amount of distraction is best.

I didn't have any problem sharing all my bad behavior and the ugly stories of my past because I had learned from Laura S that the therapist is always on the patient's side. I did not fear being judged and knew Dr. VK's only concern was to help me. She was not my friend, however. She was my therapist.

Being painfully honest worked well for me in therapy. Success in analysis comes from giving the whole, unedited, unabridged story, from beginning to end, self-fault and all. Just like following driving directions to a new place, if you leave out three steps, you will not reach your destination.

Each week, I would begin to "report" whatever was on my mind in a linear storyline, but I would soon take off on tangents, bouncing from topic to topic, including any dreams I'd had. By the end of the hour, what seemed like a random bunch of thoughts from my past, present, and subconscious would somehow come together for an amazing revelation.

I stayed committed and focused, and spent the next four years discovering, uncovering, and learning about my life and the world around me. Analyzing my life was fascinating yet very confusing. I also saw incredible contradictions from my childhood, but I had extraordinary breakthroughs.

I discovered that I had enormous anger of which I was previously unaware. I even started taking an antidepressant in the spring of 2002, because the material we were uncovering was so painful and difficult. I stayed on the medication for four years.

I found out that I wasn't wrong. I hadn't been imagining things or making them up. I did actually have a difficult childhood, and everything was not my fault. I needed to sort through my past so I would not recreate it with my children. I learned that parents, too, need boundaries. I learned that children are intuitive and sensitive from birth, and that small repetitive trauma, like never being seen or heard can actually have devastating, long-term effects.

I learned that, in alcoholic family systems, the primary relationship is with the alcohol, not the people. I learned that we are subconsciously attracted to partners who reflect our own level of life experience because our neuroses match. I was surprised by these revelations and they made me legitimately angry. I discovered that I had been stepped on and made to feel wrong.

I was so intrigued by what I was learning in therapy that I told my friends about it. I could sense their discomfort, but I couldn't help myself. I was bursting at the seams from my discoveries. My parents were silent and uncomfortable. They could see my attitude toward them changing. I would mention Dr. VK in passing and could tell by their reaction that they blamed therapy for my new behavior.

However, my kids had to come first. I could no longer worry about the adults. I was determined to pivot, to stop our generational family dysfunction, and to take my kids forward on a healthy, new trajectory. I became committed to giving them a life of openness, balance, and honest communication in which adult players would be expected to take ownership of their behavior and responsibility for their actions, or else they would not be allowed to play in our game.

I learned that we gravitate to the familiar, even if it's wrong. I had been conditioned from childhood that emotional stinginess and emotional unavailability in relationships was normal–I cannot believe how many of those relationships I had. It all fell into place one day when Dr. VK said, "Lisa, why are you going to the desert for a drink of water?"

That was an important lesson. So I steered away from people who were unbalanced, unsupportive, or judgmental, regardless of our previous relationship. If someone caused me self-doubt, or if I felt unjustly criticized by them I stepped aside. My mission never waivered–no matter what happened, nothing was going to get in my way. I was going to figure it out. I was going to make something good come from the nightmare of 9/11.

. . .

Dr. VK and I dug in and peeled back the layers. It was about understanding "why," not placing blame. It was about exposing and identifying the root causes of my issues. It was about dissecting relationship dynamics. We've all heard the analogy of peeling an onion, but in my opinion, an onion doesn't have nearly enough layers. Instead, I prefer the analogy of unwinding a big ball of string.

Imagine that everyday emotional experiences create new layers on that ball of string. A person's mental and emotional perspective at the time of the experience records that new layer–whether it is a good piece or a bad piece. This emotional recording continues to shape the psyche. Each layer is then sealed over the next day by new experiences. As time goes on, the ball of string grows and is formed, just as the psyche is uniquely shaped and defined, for better or for worse.

Now imagine an untreated emotional trauma (one large or many small, repetitive slights) as a sore becoming trapped under the layers of other emotional experiences. For the person suffering, that sore begins to fester, getting more and more inflamed. This can cause depression (anger turned inward) and/or personality issues.

The people who deny their culpability just want you to move on; they can't understand why you can't "just get over it." As the denial from those who caused the problem continues, rage in the sufferer builds to the point of bursting. They say you're being "too sensitive." By denying your feelings and not taking responsibility for their part in the situation they invalidate what you know to be true. This makes you feel crazy and doubt yourself.

Everyone was always "so surprised" when I would explode. They would metaphorically point their fingers and call me "crazy." This was the outcome of my experience of *denial*.

When you verbalize and openly examine your life events in therapy, it allows those emotional layers to begin to unravel and be discarded. In most cases, once identified, expressed, and analyzed, they simply dissolve into the atmosphere. Once processed, you often can't remember the specifics of an issue that had once been very intense when you think back on it weeks or months later.

Dr. VK explained to me that a damaged ego is like an uninsulated wire. My ego was completely exposed, therefore I was highly reactive. She helped me to believe in myself and develop a healthy self-esteem that evolved into a sense of self-love I had never known. Dr. VK calmed me down and leveled my reactive behavior. She helped me piece together the intricate puzzle that was my self, considering my point of view, acknowledging my feelings without judgment, and supporting me unconditionally, all along the way.

•   •   •

Doing psychotherapy with Dr. VK was like studying for a doctorate in Figuring Life Out.

I had to be kind to myself to do this work. I had to give myself permission. Self-kindness is a special and necessary practice unto itself. I have always been kind to others, but it has taken years to learn to give that same kindness to myself.

I had been raised in a family of conditional love. If I did not conform to their way of thinking and to the social structure in which they believed, love would be withheld. The message I received was that to ask for anything, or refer to myself, meant that I was selfish. I sought validation only from outside of myself. I was never taught by anyone to trust what I knew.

As I unraveled the layers of my life, new pieces of old stories were revealed. I would try to explain them with as much honesty and detail as I could remember. Certain topics, events, and experiences stayed with me for a long time. I learned that if something lingered in my mind, it needed more time and attention. There is an enormous amount of repetition in therapy because it is in the nuance of the retelling that the root themes emerge.

I have often told Dr. VK that I don't know how she could stand listening to me tell the same things over and over again. As a skillful practitioner, she always patiently encouraged me to keep going, knowing that with each telling, a new facet would be identified, and I would gain deeper understanding. My refracted lens would become clearer, and my life more into focus.

• • •

In the early years of therapy, I would ask Dr. VK, "How will I know when I have achieved mental health? Does a bell go off? Will they notify me by mail? What happens?"

She would answer matter-of-factly, "You will experience a rush of creative energy unlike anything you have ever known. You will have better relationships and a greater capacity to work and play. All the energy that goes into destructive pathology will now be available for creativity."

I thought to myself, *Woohoo! I'm finally going to paint! Acrylics, oils, watercolors—I can't wait! I will paint landscapes and still lifes. It's a dream come true!*

• • •

About two and a half years into therapy, Dr. VK sighed and, in a somewhat frustrated tone, said, "Lisa, we can't finish your therapy until we get your father out of the room, and we can't get your father out of the room until you stop drinking."

Hmmmm, I thought. *I should probably listen to her.*

But, still, I did not stop drinking.

Dr. VK had explained many times that alcohol and drugs alter brain chemistry. They, in effect, anesthetize old memory and it is from old, early memory that deep analysis is done. The snips of memory from early childhood are the final layers to unravel to find the foundational aspects of a person's life. Only once these are revealed can you put your feet on the ground and find the bottom from which you can build your life back up.

* * *

At the time of Teddy's death I had a consistent, nightly wine habit. Drinking had always been our social sport. We threw Dark & Stormy-themed parties everywhere we lived. As a sailor, Ted grew up drinking after races. I often thought that sailing was really just an excuse to drink. In our lives during the '80s and '90s, going out after work four or five nights a week was considered normal. On nights when we were at home, we drank some type of alcohol; this, too, had been normal in my family life growing up.

I started drinking in high school when the drinking age was eighteen and we could get into bars at sixteen. (This was not unusual in the 1970s on the Jersey Shore.) There were parties every weekend, and our culture was permeated by alcohol. College, too, seemed like one continuous party.

I didn't drink when I was pregnant with my children, but I missed it badly. But after the kids were born, I had a beer every day because it was said to increase the production of breast milk. I embraced this with gusto and looked forward to my daily beer.

By the time we moved to New Jersey, I was with kids 24/7 and thinking about my evening glass(es) of wine got me through the day. Ted wouldn't get home until eight o'clock or so. I would try to wait for him, but often I would open the bottle beforehand.

I could never have just one glass of wine. I had to have at least two and it took conscious effort to not have the third. And these weren't small glasses, either. Two glasses was half the bottle. Ted would not always join me during the week. He was more of a binge drinker, imbibing when he went out with clients and on the weekends.

My kids were not good sleepers, and I didn't sleep through the night for what seemed like ten straight years. Although sleep deprived, I would be okay in the morning but felt just south of good. I'm sure the subtle hangover I had did not help my already frustrated disposition. I blamed my irritation and my lack of satisfaction on the drudgery of motherhood, but I'm sure the wine and my guilt about drinking was another culprit.

After Teddy died, I justified having wine as the only adult thing I could do that I didn't have to share with my children.

By September of 2004, I was in the thick of managing the kids with three completely different schedules. I was digging through so much in therapy that my emotions were all over the place. By then, I was planning my life around my wine more than ever. I would wake up each morning and tell myself I wasn't going to drink that day. But by five o'clock, I would say, "What the hell" and open a bottle.

That went on for a while. Next, I told myself I wasn't going to drink at home—that I would drink only when I was out for dinner or at a friend's house. Then I found myself going to friends' houses with a bottle of wine, or I would take the kids out to dinner and have wine there. When I finally faced the music, it was clear that I had a habit I could not control by myself.

About three months after Dr. VK had told me to stop, I was having a particularly difficult week. The kids were in bed, and I was sitting alone, drinking wine by myself. The phone rang, and it was my friend Mary, a dynamic woman I had worked with in New York. We had not spoken for more than a year.

Mary had stopped drinking during our radio days, when we were in our late twenties. This was incredible to me at the time because she was the only "sober" person I knew who was my age. Somehow, she had been able to stop drinking in the heart of the 1980s, when the operative phrase was, "Let's party!"

Even in my late twenties, I knew deep down that I probably had a problem with alcohol. I wasn't drinking out of my coffee cup in the morning, but when work was over, I couldn't wait to have cocktails and to let loose. Even though I was fully functional the next day and never missed work, I thought about my drinking often (yes, this is a sign). I also knew I was on a collision course with destiny because of my father and the generational alcoholism on both sides of my family. But I could never imagine myself stopping; I loved it way too much (yes, another sign). As I got older, my go-to drinks were chardonnay in the summer and merlot in the winter. Wine wasn't that bad, right? Of course, Dark & Stormies and some other fun cocktails would sneak in there, too.

I had seen Mary the summer before when she had invited us to their weekend place on Long Island. Being sober, she and her husband didn't have liquor or wine in the house. She was long past having any issues with temptation; it was just not part of their lifestyle. I remember the first evening sheepishly telling Mary that I was going to the store to buy some wine. She didn't stop me, but I knew she had a wisdom that I did not yet share.

On the phone that night (she called out of the blue), I explained my situation to Mary. I was honest and forthright.

Mary listened attentively and then said, "Okay Lise—go downstairs and finish that bottle of wine. Then get up tomorrow, and go to an AA meeting."

Which is exactly what I did.

Having grown up in an alcoholic household, I had a lot to dig through. My time with Dr. VK was my basis for learning, but she also encouraged me to go to Alcoholics Anonymous (AA) and work the Twelve-Step Program.

Developed in 1935, AA was founded in spiritual awareness and character development. Anonymity is a key component of why AA works. You are sworn to secrecy about who is there and what is said, so there is no unnecessary or added shame. The most important theme of AA is to acknowledge that you are powerless over alcohol. You then let go of control to a Higher Power. You stand up in a room full of strangers and say, "Hi. My name is _____, and I am an alcoholic"—at which point everyone in the room echoes, "Hi, _____." I actually found this quite charming.

While it felt awkward walking into my first meeting, I was immediately overwhelmed by a wave of loving, supportive energy. I wept for the entire hour. Everyone there was connected through this common (humiliating) denominator of being powerless over alcohol; we were equals, regardless of social status, race, religion, or gender, and no one was judging. Being together as humble, imperfect humans created a remarkable spiritual connection between us. For the first time, I experienced the true meaning of fellowship.

I attended AA meetings regularly for four months. I read the books and worked the twelve steps but did not seek out a sponsor. I was very fortunate and knew how lucky I was to have private therapy.

Within the first few meetings, I learned about letting go to a Higher Power and realized that Mary's call had come from exactly that—a Higher Power. A force greater than me was helping to orchestrate my life for the better, just as it had been doing since the morning of 9/11.

From this spiritual understanding, I realized there were no coincidences. Mary's call was clearly meant to be. This new, enlightened awareness was my reward for taking the risk of becoming vulnerable. I allowed this new understanding to wash over me and my world shifted on its axis.

Once I made up my mind to quit drinking, I never looked back. I am strong-willed by nature, which can be a blessing and a curse. In this case, it was a blessing. Supported by excellent emotional guidance, I had the willpower and motivation to quit cold-turkey. I haven't had a sip of anything alcoholic since September 2004.

I no longer suffered guilt in the mornings, nor did I lose sleep unnecessarily. I did not worry about the extra calories, nor did I throw care to the wind and eat late at night. By quitting, I have broken the generational chain of alcoholism in my family. Next to analysis, stopping drinking is the single most important thing I have ever done.

The first few years after I quit drinking were socially awkward. My friends were uncomfortable around me. I had to figure out how to be in the world in this new way.

I had been drinking for twenty-five years, and the activities around it took up a lot of time. I found the habit of my social life was as hard to break as the addiction itself. I had to find some new friends. I had anticipated that the social discomfort would be hard, and it definitely was. But I was able to tolerate it, and, in the long run, the benefit has far outweighed the small price I had to pay. Life is so much better here on the other side.

They say you quit drinking when you hit the bottom. I was lucky to have a high bottom. I still cannot trust myself to have just one glass of wine, so this is how I justify it to myself: I was born with "X" number of eggs in my ovaries, and "X" number of glasses of wine. I've just had them all.

* * *

In January of 2005, to fill the gap left by my new sobriety, I went to yoga. At that time, yoga was just emerging on the East Coast. I had never tried it but had always thought it sounded interesting, if not a little weird. But I'm a little weird, so I thought, *What the hell?*

There was a beautiful yoga studio in the beach town across the bridge from where we lived. I dedicated Tuesday and Thursday mornings to my new practice. I didn't even know when I started that it was called "a practice," but in the Eastern philosophies, there is no perfection; everything is a practice. The teacher (yogi/guru) who owned the studio was from New Zealand, and he had the coolest accent ever. I was enthralled as he taught us from his vast knowledge of Sanskrit (Hindu, Buddhist from 600 BC), the poses (*asanas*), breathing techniques (*pranayama*), guided meditations (*Yoga Nidra*), visualizations, chanting, and, of course, ohm-ing, (*aum*-ing) the vibrational (primordial) sound of the universe. I seriously love ohm-ing.

Yoga taught me to be kind to myself and listen to my body; some days I felt loose, some days tight. No one was watching me, and no one was judging. It was about honoring myself for taking the time to be on my mat, doing my practice. The emotional peace and mental stimulation that yoga provided was just the healthy substitute I needed.

For the first time in my Type-A life, I did not try to control things by becoming a yoga teacher or studying it in some formal way. Instead I just let it wash over me. By letting go, I was basking in this fantastic new world and beginning to learn to just "be."

Yoga shares the message that humility and gratitude lead to living a peaceful and balanced life. I had also learned this in AA. Eastern philosophy teaches that the soul is expansive and infinite. We are temporarily in these physical bodies but eternal beings in a vast and infinite universe. My thinking shifted as I thought about the ratio of one hundred years (a human lifetime) to fourteen billion years (the age of the universe). I was humbled when I realized how small and inconsequential we really are.

Although ancient, the Eastern philosophies can be applied to our lives today.

Most importantly, Eastern philosophy also teaches about a Higher Power—the guidance and understanding of the collective soul (Spirit, God, or Universe)—and how we can tap into it at any time through meditation.

I learned that our true purpose here on beautiful Mother Earth is to live a joyful life filled with love, kindness, and light. I came to the understanding that when we let go and allow things to happen, instead of trying to force them, we attract what we want and what we want comes to us. When we are humble and satisfied with less, we receive magnificent gifts. When we trust that we are part of a greater plan with a higher purpose, we can let go and watch with confidence as life unfolds before us. When we stay in the moment and embrace the journey, we are no longer attached to the outcome.

• • •

I was in my third year of analysis. I had quit drinking. I was practicing yoga. These three steps would positively alter the course of my life, and my children's lives, forever for the better.

I continued weekly sessions with Dr. VK, gaining micro-enlightenments and "a-ha!" moments with regularity. Timmy was now three years old and beginning preschool; we had made it through the baby years. Jen was ten and Billy was seven and both kids were in elementary school. As I had predicted to myself on the morning of 9/11, life had taken on a "new normal," however, now I was a much different person.

I was a better, calmer parent. I was careful to hear and see my children as the individuals they are and to respond to their unique needs accordingly. I saw them as little seeds that had been planted. It was my job to tend the soil, feed and water them well, and make sure they had lots of clean air and sunlight so they could bloom and flourish into the best versions of themselves. I had learned to love them unconditionally.

My instinct as a mother and my new understanding about boundaries gave me the strength and courage to protect my kids from bitter, negative energy and potentially erratic behavior.

I saw how analysis had opened my mind and had clarified my misunderstandings. I was learning how things were actually supposed to work. Since childhood, I had been looking for the right answers and the proper footing. Things were finally making sense.

I attempted to separate from several difficult relationships, and while I did it imperfectly, I tried my best. My family did, too. After several turbulent years, my parents and I stopped speaking to each other except for the obligatory conversations to organize the kid's week-long visits in the summers or details around the holidays.

Having never had the choice to meet my father's side of the family, I felt it was important to not block access between my children and my parents. As difficult as it was to share my kids and be "tolerated" by my parents so they could see them, I knew it was the right thing to do. Although I know they loved my kids, I'm afraid that the love between my parents and me was almost extinguished.

BEING SEEN—WHY 9/11 HEALED ME

The strength and true essence of my warrior's will and the unconditional love and positive, consistent support from the outside world gave me the motivation to keep going. I was free, I was out of the box, and I was on a mission. I was seeing more and more of the light between the cracks.

I had finally been seen and heard enough by Dr. VK that the desperate insecurities I had suffered in my life began to recede. Just to have my thoughts acknowledged and not contradicted at every turn was refreshing.

The *kindness of strangers* in our lives never wavered. Since 9/11, the positive attention and unconditional love I have been given from friends and neighbors, my community and country, as well as strangers around the world has filled my empty cup and allowed me to heal.

• • •

Studying my own life has been the most interesting thing I have ever done. The reward of emotional well-being is to feel confident, balanced, and grounded instead of trying to find solid footing in quicksand. The rumination I was plagued with twenty-four hours a day by the time Ted died is now gone. That nasty voice in my head has been muzzled.

I now understand what it means to set appropriate boundaries so that everyone is happy or at least they know the rules so that I am happy. When my daughter was small, I would hear the idea of boundaries referenced all the time. I remember thinking to myself, *What in the hell's a "boundary?"* It took 9/11 for me to figure it out. And it turns out the boundaries most needed were not for my children but for the adults in my life. Who knew?

Since 9/11, I am far more considerate as a parent and a much better friend. The wisdom I gained by studying every aspect of my life over the past seventeen years has delivered my children and me to a place I could have only imagined. My study has shown me the light between the cracks of 9/11 and has made me better for having lived it.

PERFECT IMPERFECTION–HEALED BUT NEVER CURED

"Therapy is the springboard that unlocks in a person what is already there."—Dr. VK.

While I am healed, I will never be completely cured. I am now self-aware enough and have the skills to navigate away from triggers, situations, or relationships that could pull me off course. Being present and mindful in daily life is a constant practice through which I see the value of living a conscious life with a focus on kindness to myself as much as to others. That once exposed wire that was my ego is now well insulated. Dr. VK calls this being "emotionally inoculated."

I feel fortified with knowledge and firmly planted on a solid, emotionally-educated foundation. Much of my refracted view has been corrected, and I now see life through a far clearer lens. I am grateful to have an emotional skillset to manage almost anything.

I am no longer reactive. I now surround myself with "a moat of objectivity" that allows me a moment's pause to stop and consider the situation before I respond. This has helped me to become steady and wise counsel for my children and friends.

I have learned what it means to fully love myself, and that self-love means loving the bad as much if not more than the good. The good stuff is easy to love, but the bad stuff, seen right, can be great, too. In fact it has been embracing my imperfections that has brought me into balance. I have put shame and self-punishment behind me. I do my best every day to be the best person I can be and forgive myself the rest.

As I had hoped, analysis led me to figure out the "why" of many, many things. I highly recommend emotional counseling and mental-health therapy. The world is a complicated place, and we are complex and sensitive creatures. We are not born knowing all the answers. We need to learn new skills and to have an empathetic understanding of ourselves and others, to not only to survive but to thrive, *sur-thrive,* in our new world.

CHAPTER NINE

REACHING THE LIGHT

An Existential Breakthrough and
Cozmeena Enlightened Living

It was November of 2005, fourteen months after I had stopped drinking, and I was on the couch in Dr. VK's office. One of us said something that I can't remember now but in a sudden, surreal moment, all the pieces of the puzzle fell into place. I broke through the ceiling to mental health and received a rush of creative energy unlike anything I had ever known.

I sat bolt upright and exclaimed, "OMG!! Do we want Armageddon, or do we want *The Jetsons*?" Meaning, "Do we want the end of the world, or do we want a future of brilliant possibilities? All we have to do is *be nice*! It's so simple!"

"We are all far more similar than we are different! Peel off our outer layer, and we all look the same! This life is a blip on the screen in the scheme of the universe, and we should be enjoying it instead of taking everything so seriously. We can have peace and love instead of death and destruction. People are inherently good. All we have to do is shift our focus to see it. We can do this! We have this choice! It is so simple!"

In this existential moment of enlightenment, I saw things clearly. I saw the light, and I understood. It felt like I was standing on solid ground, having found my footing for the first time in my life.

My friends and I were mothers of school-aged children with busy lives, running around, taking care of our families but taking very little care of ourselves. In the next moment of clarity I said: "Wait! Who is taking care of mothers? Who is taking care of women? Who is taking care of the caregiver? And what caregiver doesn't need care?"

When Dr. VK described the creative download that would come, I had fantasized that I would paint fine art. But no, it was nothing like that.

I had always loved and excelled at any type of crafting: knitting, sewing, crocheting, and baking. Of course, crafting would be the way my creative outlet would surface. So, I started knitting like a fiend. With my hands actively engaged in this soothing, tactile meditation, I could think and process. Everything made so much sense. I was figuring "it" out.

"It" was about kindness, love, and respect, consideration, grace, and decency. "It" was about seeing that we are far more similar than we are different—equal as human beings regardless of background. "It" was about treating others in the ways we wanted to be treated. "It" was about recognizing our basic human need for emotional warmth, comfort, and care and understanding how essential that need really is.

* * *

I was compelled to create and craft with my hands. Doing so calmed my mind and soothed my soul as I rode this incredible wave. I learned later that tactile activities—or anything that uses your fingertips such as knitting—can physiologically calm the central nervous system and quiet the mind.

Through my sense of touch, I was tapping into my creative, intuitive right-brain, giving my logical, analytical left-brain a rest. It was in this space that I could see things so differently and solutions would come.

As I was knitting, I reprocessed my life. The enlightened "breakthrough" had come when I had unraveled enough layers and analyzed enough experiences that I could find the foundation of when my misunderstanding had begun. With this new clarity, I reviewed the experiences, events, and relationships in my life and everything began to make sense. From this new vantage point, I could rethink the events of my life and relearn them in the right way.

Everything Dr. VK had said about clearing away the destructive pathology that was taking up so much mental time and space was true. Now I had a clear channel to see the world without the twists and turns of negative, self-destructive distraction.

Knitting wasn't "something I thought I should do"—it was a true calling. I was being guided and inspired to create something beautiful, tangible, and warm for all my women friends, to care for them with loving thanks for all they had done for me. I could sense the ones who were struggling and needed help themselves (because who doesn't?).

So I began to take care of "other mothers"—by knitting for them.

I derived the pattern from a shawl that I had bought as a gift for Ted's mother and began to knit large, triangular, wool shawls using thick, gorgeous yarn on big, fat needles. The knitting went very fast. I could finish one in about twelve hours or two weeks of evening television when the kids were sleeping.

The shawl had a sincere yet lighthearted essence. It was something to throw on over your pajamas to drive the kids to school so that you would look dressed and beautiful from the waist up. The best part was that no one would know your secret.

I would choose a special color that I thought would flatter the specific friend who was next on my list. I would sit in the evening and knit, infusing my love into each stitch as I thought of that dear friend and the times we'd shared together—her life, her humor, her beauty, and our friendship. If she was hurting I would send strength and positive thoughts to her as well. I thought about her reaction when I gave it to her and how beautiful she would look with it on. I was excited for her to feel the warm embrace and caring comfort it would give her when she wore it. It was my heartfelt, metaphoric "hug," my personal gift of thanks and love that would care for her in this special way.

I couldn't stop. I couldn't control it, and I didn't want to. Yes, it was crazy, but the greatest kind of crazy.

The choice of who to knit for generally came in a random order but, of course, the first shawl went to Dr. VK. Who takes care of the therapist, right? The second shawl went to Bar Scott, my beautiful, singer-songwriter friend from the *Voices of Inspiration Concert* who had lost her young son. The third shawl I knitted was for my friend and neighbor, Carol, who is a very special woman. She is lovely, nurturing, witty, smart, very funny, and, oh, she is beautiful. She has a warm inner glow and a humorous, charming energy that makes you feel special just by being near her.

One cold Sunday morning in early February 2006, I went to Carol's house and found her in the kitchen with her family. I walked in wearing this big, thick, winter white wool shawl, took it off, and wrapped it around her, in my "special way." She was stunned. The family gathered around and could not believe that I had made this beautiful gift for her. My heart swelled with warmth and love as I watched her sheer delight in receiving it. She looked gorgeous even with her bedhead hair and flannel jammies.

As she turned around in her playful joy, she exclaimed, "Oh, my gosh! It's so warm! It's so cozy! It's like a great, big hug!" Then she twirled again, caught a glimpse of herself in the mirror, and stopped. Taking a big, dramatic breath, she exclaimed, ". . . but it's so beautiful! It's like a Pashmina! No! It's a *Cozmeena*!"

Carol repeated again. "It's a *Cozmeena*. It's where coziness meets glamour!" The shawl combined the beautiful allure and simple elegance of a Pashmina wrap with the wonderful warmth, comfort, and care of a mother's loving hug.

When I heard Carol say *Cozmeena*, I loved it. The idea resonated in every cell of my body. So the name stuck and the *Cozmeena* Shawl was born.

For the next two years, I enjoyed an incredible, manic ride of revelation, enlightenment, and awareness that I could have imagined only in my wildest dreams. I wanted to tell the world. I wanted everyone to "have what I had" and to learn what I now knew. I had seen the light. It was big and huge and manic and crazy. I wanted to shout it from the rooftops. It was fantastic. It was good. And my sincerest and greatest wish was that everyone in the world could experience "it," too.

I felt like Wile E. Coyote riding the Acme rocket in the 1960s "Road Runner" cartoons, flying forward at a screaming pace. I was having so much fun I could hardly stand it. I know I sounded crazy but I didn't care. I felt that I held the key to saving humankind and having peace on earth.

All we had to do was be nice. Be kind. Do unto others. Live the Golden Rule. That was it!

* * *

COZMEENA

In the months that followed my breakthrough, during this remarkable creative window, the concept of a new lifestyle platform began to come into focus. The ideas flowed from me with an effortless, natural grace and I spent my days thinking of all the ways they could be applied. The more I thought about it the more I saw the simple solution of how we could bring more joy, balance, and happiness to ourselves and others and make the world a better place.

I began to call the concept *Cozmeena* because the name just worked. It was the philosophical continuation of the same expansive, loving energy that motivated me to make the shawls. Multidimensional ideas of what *Cozmeena* could be grew in my mind with each passing day.

What if we could live lives based on consideration, grace, and decency? What if we could live in a place where the human, sensory needs were a priority for all? What if our state of mind was to consciously live in the moment, acknowledging and helping our fellow human beings by spreading love and genuine kindness from the heart? I tried to think of how best to explain it. The only word that seemed to work was "enlightenment." *Cozmeena* enlightenment.

I could imagine so many paths to attain a *Cozmeena* enlightened life:

- ♥ Actualizing *Cozmeena* enlightenment in your day would mean that you would mindfully greet those you pass on the street, acknowledging them with a smile and respectful hello. It was not to seek a deep friendship or have a long conversation, but to give a positive moment of acknowledgment that they exist and they matter–it was to behave with common decency.

- ♥ A *Cozmeena* moment would be when you recognize and care for the needs of another without the expectation of receiving thanks or recognition. The reward is the self-appreciation gained by knowing that you have extended genuine, heart-centered kindness to another. It is understanding that caring for others nurtures your heart and fills your soul, which gives you a warm and peaceful sense of satisfaction and self-love.

- ♥ *Cozmeena* would be a place of *personal power,* where conflict resolution is founded on the mutual agreement to respectfully agree to disagree and move forward in a positive, parallel way without needing to dominate, win, or control. It would be about having respectful consideration of others, being introspective about your own behavior, and seeing a situation from the other person's point of view.

♥ Living a *Cozmeena* lifestyle would be understanding that human beings gain self-comfort and care through any of the five senses: taste, touch, sight, smell, and sound.

Even more importantly it would be where you use your sixth sense (intuition) when making life choices. *Cozmeena* would be when you understand to trust your inner guidance system, above all else, to navigate your life.

I fantasized, "*What if we were able to coexist, side-by-side, living together with respectful decency and graceful consideration of each other? What would our world look like then?*"

These concepts were neither unique nor original. They could be found in philosophies and religions that speak of love and kindness, doing unto others, living in the moment, and viewing life as a gift. The most important common denominator being the acknowledgment of a Higher Power.

I saw *Cozmeena* as a twenty-first-century version of these philosophies. In addition, not only did I see the light of these simple, heartfelt concepts but by the time I was finished, I had thought of many tactical ways to feel better by using sensory input to nurture our hearts. I could also see how to sort and curate content that already existed to share and propagate the message. Here was a way to utilize the resources of our contemporary, new world while bringing forward the timeless wisdom of the old.

As the years passed, the definition of *Cozmeena* became clearer. It would mean living your life in the moment with conscious, heart-centered balance, gratitude, humility, and grace. It would be where there was no judgment or criticism of yourself or others, and kindness would be the Golden Rule. It would be where you see life through a lens of love instead of through a lens of fear; and when you would understand and let go, enjoying your time on the planet because you know it is a fleeting and beautiful gift.

Living a *Cozmeena* lifestyle would also mean facing life with courage, knowing the lessons lie within the struggle, to reframe pain as a catalyst for personal growth, and to have resilience, fortitude, and perseverance to push through the obstacles. It would mean to stay on the path and to be more aware of the journey than attached to the outcome. It would mean looking for—and finding—the light between the cracks in all difficult experiences.

THE POCKET HEART

In the first days after 9/11, I was frantically looking for Ted. While there was nothing I could really do, I still did everything possible. At 5:00 AM on September 12, when I was up nursing Timmy, I called every hospital in the 411 Information Directory in New York and Jersey City to see if they had any unidentified victims.

I didn't expect much, because, in the middle of the night, I had turned on the news, which showed Emergency Room entrances of area hospitals, with staff and gurneys waiting, but there were no cars on the road. There was not a person in sight. I watched and watched but not a soul was coming.

I can still remember having this driving need to get into the city to look for Ted. I felt frantic, even though, in my logical mind, I knew he probably would never be found. The intense angst and pressure was nagging and constant. I was frustrated beyond description that I couldn't abandon my responsibilities and go there, but there was nothing I could do to change my situation.

The pleading hope of the friends around me, and a grain of hope I held within, made me consider all possibilities, because nothing had been confirmed.

I asked our friend Jim, a dear friend of Ted's from college who had been an usher in our wedding, to check the morgues around the city. Jim stoically accepted the mission. He had lost Ted and several other friends.

I asked another friend who lived in the city to go to the television stations with Ted's photograph because they were showing missing people on the news. I knew in my heart this endeavor was pointless, but I went through the motions anyway, because that's what you do; you never give up.

Two mornings after 9/11, I was standing in my busy kitchen with a dozen or so people milling around. A friend that I recognized from church came in unexpectedly. I was surprised to see him, since we didn't know each other that well.

Stanley was the Fire Chief and Borough Administrator in the next town over. He walked in quietly and stood next to me with his hands in his pockets. As he looked down at me, I looked up and saw that he was clearly upset and fighting his emotions. Then, with a deep breath he stood up straight and regained his strong demeanor.

Slowly, he pulled his hand out of his pants pocket and said to me sincerely in a quiet voice, "Lisa, I went to Ground Zero yesterday looking for Teddy. I had this with me, and I want you to have it." He opened his hand to reveal a small, silver, coin-like medal with a winged angel embossed on it. "It's a pocket angel," he said.

When I touched the pocket angel to take it from his hand, a wave of dizziness and rush of tingles coursed through my body. I felt connected to Ground Zero. Just like a *port key* from the Harry Potter series–it was as if I had been magically transported to the site. In that instant, a sense of calm washed over me, and the pressure to get into the city suddenly dissipated. I no longer had to go; it was as if I had already been there.

I truly believe that the pocket angel was mystical. It allowed me to get to Ground Zero in my own time. Although tiny in size, the pocket angel is the single most astonishing gift I received throughout my 9/11 experiences. It is one of the core, foundational elements of *Cozmeena* kindness.

One spring day in 2006, my kids and I were playing with polymer baking clay. Because the pocket angel had meant so much to me, I was inspired to make *Pocket Hearts*—something whimsical in memory of Teddy's lighthearted love and playful spirit. Over the next few months, I perfected the technique of twisting, folding, and pinching the clay into the shape of a heart. The *Pocket Heart* became my favorite way of sharing the love that my kids and I have received since 9/11.

Since 2006, I have been sharing *Pocket Hearts* by pulling them out of my pocket and holding them in the palm of my hand, just as Stanley did when he gave me the pocket angel. I go through my day passing them out randomly to friends and strangers as they cross my path.

I say, "Please take a *Pocket Heart* for luck and love." And in the next moment, with a wink and a smile I say, "Don't be surprised—they're a little magic, too."

Over the years I have received hundreds of charming and beautiful stories about *Pocket Hearts*. People say that when they find them—in jacket pockets from the season before, in the bottom of their purse, or in the well of their car console—it always gives them a lift and makes them smile. People have held them through surgery, when babies were being born, while taking tests, and while traveling to distant places.

It is very interesting how men respond. Sometimes they're a little gruff when they take them, but months later, I learn that they never leave home without it.

Although people want to buy the *Pocket Hearts,* I know that selling them would mess with their magic. However, there are plans to develop a *Pocket Heart* kit in the future, so that people can make their own.

Like knitting, playing with clay is not just fun for me; it is a functional meditation. When I'm not knitting, you'll find me making *Pocket Hearts,* as I've been doing since 2006.

The *Pocket Heart* is a tangible metaphor and daily reminder of the wonder and beauty, the unparalleled love, support, and kindness, the patriotism and unity, and the resilience of the human spirit that is the Godness of 9/11.

As of this writing, there are more than 40,000 *Pocket Hearts* circulating in the world today. It is my hope that one day all the *Pocket Hearts* will connect, as seeds of love, bringing together like-minded people in a gentle, lighthearted Kindness Revolution.

PUTTING COZMEENA ON HOLD

Two years into my enlightened experience, my mind began to slow down. Wile E. Coyote and the Acme rocket had finally run out of gas. I had exhausted every conceivable angle of the *Cozmeena* vision I could think of.

During the months of discovery, I had had such a clear vision for our beautiful future that I wanted to shout it from the rooftops. I felt I had solutions for how to feel better, both tactically and philosophically. I wanted everyone to know what I had learned, to have what I had, and to see what I saw.

Even though I knew it would take years to realize my vision, I really thought that I could do it. But when I would try to explain my ideas to my friends, they would politely nod their heads and humor me. Then after a few minutes, their eyes would glaze over, and I knew I'd lost them. There were a special few that listened and understood, but to the world at large, the *Cozmeena* concept was so vast and metaphysical, that to explain it clearly and in less than an hour was impossible. So when no one could listen to me anymore and I started sounding crazy even to myself, I took the hint and put it away. But that was okay. I soon realized that this crazy manic ride of reprocessing my life had been necessary for me to be able to quiet down and just "be."

Dr. VK soothed my disappointed ego. "Lisa, Mother Teresa said you can affect only those along your path." When I heard this initially, it made me mad. But when I came down to earth I embraced it.

I continued making *Pocket Hearts*, giving them out at every opportunity. I continued knitting *Cozmeena* Shawls for the women who crossed my path. I baked *Cozmeena* Granola and other yummy comfort foods to share them with family and friends. I enjoyed my life living in the here and now no longer consumed by the past or focused on the future. I snuggled in with my kids and basked in the moment, content in my incredible life. I had been on such a manic ride for so long that to be quiet and live a simple, daily life was pure pleasure.

CHAPTER TEN

A FEW CLOUDS ALONG THE WAY

Life Will Test You

Eight years after 9/11, in late January of 2009, I was talking to a friend the morning of my annual breast exam. She jokingly said, "Don't worry. You're in trouble only if they tell you to watch 'the movie'."

Lying on the table in the dark examination room, I watched on the ultrasound screen as the tech moved the wand over the same areas on my breast. The radiologist came in and looked at the two suspicious spots. I had chosen a progressive practice because their policy was to perform biopsies the same day if something was found. Knowing myself as I do if I had to wait two weeks for results of a test, I would go crazy.

The doctor did a needle aspiration of the first dark spot, and, because it was only fluid, we watched it collapse on the screen. The second area was different and required a core biopsy, in which a small piece of tissue was clipped and sent for analysis. This pathology took several days. As it was a Thursday afternoon, I had to wait through the weekend for the results.

As I was getting up from the table, the doctor said to me, "I don't like how this looks, and I'd like for you to watch an informative movie." The look on her face said it all. I had breast cancer. As I was leaving the office, she said, pragmatically, "Don't worry—you'll be fine." Not the warm and fuzzy counsel I was hoping for, but as it turns out, very true.

So, I thought, *here we go again. Let's jump on another emotional roller coaster, shall we? God! You cannot make this shit up!* My mind raced and scrambled like a video game on steroids. It pinged and lurched and banged off the walls. It processed every imaginable horrible scenario I had ever heard and a few that I hadn't. But within a couple hours, my dear friend Nature kicked in and gave me some lovely numbness. I went home and told no one.

In the days between my biopsy and the cancer confirmation, I had a realization: I was being tested. I had spent the previous seven years analyzing, studying, and learning how to be emotionally resilient, right? I wondered, *Could I have developed a skill set for trauma management?*

I really didn't know what to expect, but I braced myself for another long haul. Once again my warrior instincts kicked in, and I said to myself, *"You are strong. You are resilient. This will not take you down. If it's true, you can handle it."*

Three days later it was confirmed that I had breast cancer. My dear friend, Cindy, who had been right beside me since Ted's death, arrived unexpectedly as I was hanging up with the doctor. Talk about Divine timing. She reached out and caught me as I emotionally fell to pieces. Cindy was exactly who I needed to see in that moment, and I was sustained by her remarkable strength and calm resilience. She generously accompanied me to all my doctor appointments for moral support and to be my scribe when I couldn't trust myself to remember the specific details.

I was confident that I'd be okay, but I was really worried about my kids. I knew it would take weeks, even months, for them to process this new information. Their last remaining parent was now in peril, and "cancer" is a really scary word. My boys were still young, but I knew I would not be able to fool Jen, who was now a freshman in high school. She could grasp the concept of mortality and had been acutely tuned in to me since her father's death; now she would have to handle this. I needed time to figure out how to tell her.

But, Jen found out the next day when my gynecologist, a family friend, called at 5:40 PM and left a message on the answering machine. Jen was sitting in the next room watching television and heard the incoming message: "Lisa! I just got the report, and I'm so sorry! I will do everything I can to help you. Please call me as soon as you can!"

Jen came to find me. She said, "Mom, are you okay? Mrs. Smith just left you a message and she sounded really worried."

I couldn't believe it. *Seriously? Really? You have to be kidding me! And from a medical professional! OMG!*

But to Jen, I downplayed her message as calmly as I could, "Oh, don't worry, honey. Mrs. Smith is just a drama queen. I had a little test the other day. I'm sure it's fine. Really."

Both Jen and I were seeing Dr. VK at the time, and the following week, when I went to my appointment, the first thing she said with Jen's consent was, "Jen knows."

I was still processing the situation myself, and now I had to deal with my daughter's shock and premature stress. She had known for a week and had kept it to herself. There was no undoing the damage. The poor kid; this was too much for anyone at the age of fourteen. Jen had already lived the reality of one parent's death. As the oldest, she had taken on responsibilities far beyond her years after Ted died.

Breast cancer when detected early has a 98 percent cure rate, but even so, I knew there would be a long process ahead of me. It would be how I handled it that would make the difference. If I were strong, my kids would be strong. If I could count on anything to get us through this, it would be my newfound confidence and self-awareness.

I dreaded that my world would become a mini-9/11 when people found out. I didn't think I could handle all the attention again. I felt like I had just finished thanking everyone for their support and that life was finally back to normal. The drama of my being a 9/11 widow now diagnosed with breast cancer would be too much. My first impulse was to duck and hide, but that's not how I roll.

It was no surprise when the news got out that people jumped in to help. I never doubted they would be there. When I started chemo, friends brought dinners by for weeks. Although I was grateful, I felt that I just couldn't receive any more. To maintain balance, for every family who brought us dinner, I made a heavy loaf of Amish Friendship Bread.

I had surgery in mid-February. Billy and Timmy were still young enough that I could bluff having the flu to buy time before telling them. Billy had been suffering from night terrors caused by PTSD that had been plaguing him since the prior summer. He had awoken each night and had been coming in to sleep on the couch in my room for months. Thankfully, he was given a meaningful part in the school play that winter, which was the perfect, healthy distraction to give his mind a break, and he was finally able to quiet down. By early March, he was sleeping through the night, but it had been a dicey six months for both of us.

I wasn't due to start chemo until late April, so I was still waiting to tell the boys. However, in late March, Billy found out that I had breast cancer when the "wig lady" left a message on our answering machine. That's right. It happened again.

Understandably, he freaked out. But by then, I'd had enough time to digest everything and plan my strategy. I was able to give him examples of other moms we knew, who had had much more serious cases than mine, and were now fine. He handled the information well, and, thank God, his night terrors did not resurface. Timmy was still very young, so he was spared too much fear. I was able to downplay the situation with confidence so that he believed me.

As the months went by, I realized that I had developed a skill set for trauma management. I had let go of control and allowed the process to take its course not dwelling or overthinking my thoughts. I rode the waves of negative emotions knowing they would pass. I trusted and believed I would be okay and knew that one day (soon) it would all be behind us.

Gratefully, because of what I had learned I was able to navigate the four of us through the experience well.

There is a blood test called an "Oncotype" that predicts the percentage rate of possible recurrence and helps to determine the need for chemotherapy. Lobular cancer is aggressive, so, even though they had caught it early, when I was discussing the Oncotype test with my surgeon, she said, "You are a young woman and a single parent with three kids. Why would you risk even one cell getting out?"

So I opted for all the treatments: surgery, chemotherapy, and radiation, to be sure my cancer was completely eradicated. I have always referred to my cancer as "cancer-lite," meaning that, while I went through all the treatments, I was never fighting for my life. So while I didn't dodge the bullet, it did just graze me.

My surgery was a lumpectomy, not a mastectomy, and it was under my breast so my body appeared the same. Chemotherapy was tolerable, and radiation was easy. It was a long ten months, but, once it was finished, I never looked back. So, in reality, I cut the cancer out, poisoned it out, and burned it out; then I let it go with the peace of mind that I had done everything I could.

Native Alaskans have many words for "snow," and the French have many words for "love." I believe there should be many more words to describe the variations of cancer, because the word itself is so shocking and scary that, when you hear it, you feel like you've just heard a death sentence—even though, more often than not, that is far from the truth.

* * *

I wish I could tell you that the relationship with my parents had healed between 9/11 and my breast cancer diagnosis but unfortunately it had not. By then we had been estranged for many years so when they found out they didn't offer their help and I didn't ask. In the few conversations we did have, my parents made my breast cancer about them. After that, I just couldn't take it anymore–my patience had run out.

Cancer was my liberation. It set me free. It exposed the reality of the destructive, selfish, and toxic relationships in my life and gave me permission to walk away from them.

CHAPTER ELEVEN

LIVING IN THE LIGHT
Perfect Imperfection

I f I had simply listened to my parents or blindly followed society's traditional rules, I would never be where I am today. Four years into analysis, I woke up realizing that all we had to do was be nice. After a lifetime of feeling like no one was ever nice to me, experiencing the ongoing *kindness of strangers* enlightened me to the power of this simple action. To give and receive kindness is life changing, it is world changing, and it is incredibly easy to do. All it took for me to see it was the most catastrophic event in recent world history.

• • •

After hearing the story of my life, I hope you understand that I know my parents and those who came before them were good people who were doing their best. They loved me and gave me as much as they were capable of, but they did not have the skills to handle the emotional complexities that came with the tragic events in their lives, nor did they have the emotional training required to navigate the troubled relationships within our family.

I am happy to report that my parents and I have reconnected since our difficulties post-9/11 and that healing and forgiveness have taken place between us. Although my father died estranged from me several years ago, I have found peace, understanding, and forgiveness for us both since his death. My spiritual education has helped with this tremendously.

My mother and I have come to a place of balance after many years of difficult discussions. On a recent visit, I told her that I was finally able to let go of my need for her to validate my experience and that I appreciated her listening. I accepted that she could not take responsibility for her part in my childhood pain. She surprised me by saying, "Thank you, too, for being patient enough to continue explaining it to me until I understood."

· · ·

9/11 shot me out of the proverbial box–a box I had never fit into. Being out of that box allowed me to see the remarkable and positive light amid the chaos and darkness in which we all were immersed. This gave me the chance to pivot and shift the trajectory of my young family for the better.

I listened to my inner guidance for the first time in my life and took what turned out to be the correct path in the fork in the road. Trusting myself, following my intuition, and pushing through the struggle were key to my ultimate healing. It is through these actions that I discovered my self-love.

We each see life from a distinct vantage point influenced by our personality and life experience. We are shaped emotionally by our unique encounters of the events and relationships in our lives. I see now that what I have lived through in my life, the bad and the good, ultimately gave me the life lessons I needed to handle Teddy's death and 9/11 in the ways that I did.

I realize that there was never a choice. My life was destined to take this course so that I could be here with you telling my story with the hope of doing my small part to help make the world a better place.

CYCLE OF HEALING

From my 9/11 experience I've identified a cycle of giving and receiving. The logic to gracefully let others help you in order to help themselves is very clear to me now. If we keep others from helping us in our time of pain or crisis, we are blocking them from receiving the soul food they, too, desperately need. Human beings need to help each other. It is hardwired in our DNA.

By trying to muscle through by ourselves we make a bad experience unnecessarily more difficult and miss out on one of the most beautiful experiences of being human. When we allow ourselves to receive, we gain humility. When we let down our guard, show our vulnerability, and allow ourselves to receive, we are graced with the gift of gratitude and the understanding of what it means to be an exquisite, multidimensional, perfectly imperfect human being. How satisfying it is to live in the moment in centered balance and grateful appreciation, playing the game that is this remarkable life.

In our chaotic and unstable world–from an angry Mother Nature to devastating national and world events–it is likely that one day each of us will need help. When that happens, I encourage you to embrace the notion that not only is it good to give but it is also good to receive. This exchange is a healthy and necessary cycle of healing.

Personal struggle and collective trauma open new dimensions of wisdom and understanding. The light between the cracks of these events are the love and human connection that come from letting down our guard and rallying together. The best of humanity rises when we are pushed into action and shows up through the *kindness of strangers*. Choosing to shift our thinking and allow ourselves to show vulnerability can help to bring balance and make a beautiful change in the world.

PAIN AS A CATALYST

Trauma is a shocking opener that projects you to an entirely new place. Pain is always a part of that. Pain gets our attention, and while it can be unpleasant and scary, it is also a natural and integral part of the human experience. As difficult as it might be, allowing pain, without avoiding, denying, or medicating it too much, can lead us on a fast track to personal growth.

The pain in my life has been exactly that: a fast track to personal growth. As difficult as some of my experiences have been, I now see the profound gifts and wisdom I have gained from each of them.

When something happens, instead of asking *Why is this happening TO me*, I ask, *Why is this happening FOR me? What am I being shown? What am I supposed to learn?*

I discovered that life is my classroom and the struggles are my lessons. Advancing through them, looking inward, objectively observing, and learning from them has given me enormous wisdom and understanding and has made me who I am today.

TAKING RESPONSIBILITY

As you read my story you saw how the subtle slights I received growing up made me feel ignored, shunned, shamed, and dismissed, and while this may have seemed insignificant to those around me, it was not. Words can hurt. Actions can hurt. Inaction can hurt. Not truly seeing or hearing someone can hurt. We are all special and sensitive creatures and we each need a unique balance of proper care, communication, and consideration in order to thrive.

You learned it is never too late to take responsibility for our actions. Relationships can be mended and healed at any time. However, this does take courage. It takes courage to show vulnerability, to swallow your pride and take responsibility for the damage you've caused, whether it was intended or not.

Admitting fault is not a sign of weakness. Admitting fault is a sign of enormous strength. It also doesn't take hours–sometimes it only takes seconds. Ten seconds of courage can begin a conversation that can heal a relationship almost immediately.

Being brave and admitting fault can be transformative. When I quit drinking, the courage it took to cross the threshold at my first AA meeting and show my vulnerability was quickly rewarded with my initial understanding of humility, gratitude, and a higher power.

Taking ownership and responsibility is the basis of building trust and it has led me to living a far happier life with more loving, respectful, and satisfying relationships with those I love, including myself.

LIVING MY PERFECT IMPERFECTION

My 9/11 experiences taught me that being open-minded, considerate of others, flexible in my thinking, and curious about the world around me is the key to living a happy life.

I no longer feel the need to be emphatic or forceful about what I think or know; I no longer have to be right all the time. I am happy with myself and do not feel the need to criticize or judge others. My mind-set has shifted from *power over*—where the key is to win, dominate, and beat out the competition—to *personal power*, which involves mutually agreeing to disagree and coexisting and/or cocreating with respectful consideration of others.

9/11 taught me how to set healthy boundaries in my adult relationships. I finally have my priorities straight and give myself permission to put my own needs in line with everyone else's. I say "no" when things do not work for me and "yes" when they do. I also now understand that certain people do not belong in my life and that I can love them from afar.

I have found a formula to stay centered and balanced, which includes exercising, trying to eat right, getting massages or back adjustments every month or two, taking a candlelit bath to relax at night, staying disciplined with my meditation and work schedule, and setting realistic goals and expectations.

I've let go of things I cannot control, which is pretty much everything. I trust and allow Divine Order to have it covered. When something breaks my stride, I gracefully sidestep it and move on as best I can. I am flexible and stay in the moment with less attachment to the outcome.

In the morning, I meditate so that I am aligned with my highest self for the greatest good of my children, all others, and myself. At night I tap into my sense of touch through crafting to calm my central nervous system. These daily practices allow me to stay quiet, balanced, and emotionally flexible, in order to positively handle whatever comes my way.

As a perfectly imperfect human being, I still have daily struggles, but now I understand the process and trust it. I know that trying new things, going into unfamiliar territory, or taking any kind of risk will involve a level of discomfort. Starting new projects, like this book and all things *Cozmeena*, often puts me in this position but I know that given time, new things become familiar, then quickly routine.

I hug my broken inner child so that she knows she's still loved, even when she is bad. This is a really nice practice that I strongly encourage because we bring our broken inner child with us everywhere we go and into every interaction we have. Eight-year-old Lisa, fifteen-year-old Lisa, and many-other-aged Lisas are with me all the time interacting with the inner children of those with whom I come in contact.

I am happy to now be doing for myself what I do for others. What a pleasure to be cared for with my own gracious generosity and love. I do this not from a place of selfishness or ego, but from a place of gratitude, humility, and understanding. This continuous practice of self-kindness is a pleasure because when I am kind to myself, I am even more kind to others. Putting these ingredients together in a heartfelt recipe for a beautiful, balanced life leaves me feeling fulfilled, grounded, and joyful.

RECOGNIZING INNER WISDOM

9/11 showed me how to see the value of my life experience. I realize that I have always known more than I gave myself credit for. For years, I mistakenly looked outside of myself for validation when, in fact, no one knew what I needed except for me. I now see the value of what I've learned and enjoy a grounded, confident wisdom.

Being mindful of my shortcomings, I own my behavior and do my best to let my children and friends know what is realistic to expect from me. I remind them that I am imperfect and struggle as much as they do. Every day is a fresh start, with more to learn and new ways to grow, and I am moving forward in my life with this wisdom. I fully trust my intuition to guide me and recognize that it has been showing me the right path to take all along. All I need to do is pay attention.

My ego has moved to the back seat, and I now sit in the front in my perfect imperfection. It is so much easier to navigate life from this place of acceptance, knowing that I am faulted. After all, striving to be perfect is exhausting, not to mention impossible and really, really boring.

I learned that life prepared me for life. My life experience has given me the wisdom to better navigate everything that crosses my path. There is great value in knowing that whatever comes my way is preparing me for the future. When I encounter stormy times, I am mindful that I am gaining useful and valuable knowledge that will help me later.

I feel a new, quiet sense of personal power. My self-confidence is in beautiful balance with humility and gratitude. I have learned that going with the ebb and flow of life and staying in the moment makes me less attached to the outcome–instead I enjoy watching with curiosity and wonder as my path unfolds before me.

Learning from life's journey and finding that glimmer of joy while embracing the struggle continues to teach me the greatest lessons. It allows me to see the light between the cracks. And you can, too.

●　●　●

ACKNOWLEDGMENTS

I n my naiveté about what it takes to write a book, what I thought would take nine months ended up taking a year and a half. Two sets of editors and teachers saw me through this incredible learning curve with patience and encouragement, keeping me (semi)-sane throughout the process.

Heartfelt thanks go to my Developmental Editor, Ann Delgehausen, my book-writing guru and teacher who got me started from a completely stopped position. Ann's wisdom and tutelage supported me through the trials and errors of what is known as the first "shitty" draft (thank you Ann Lamont), and the other "shitty" drafts that followed.

Despite's Ann's leadership and support, after nine straight months of weekly discussions, outlines, drafts, writing, rewriting, editing, and jamming for eight hours a day until I couldn't see straight, I came to realize that what I had written was actually a "brain dump" and not even close to the book I wanted to write.

Despite the dozens of hours I spent in development, I couldn't seem to get the information organized nor did I have a clear vision of the story I was trying to tell. In June 2017,

I had to face the painful realization that I would not make my original deadline of the sixteenth anniversary of 9/11 in September 2017. Because I blindly jumped into writing this book in the hopes of building a speaking platform, I had no idea of the scope of the project I had undertaken. So, with plenty of kicking and cursing, I pushed the deadline off another year to September 2018 and stopped writing for the summer.

In those summer months, the ideas stewed, and perked, and processed. When the kids went back to school, I faced the project again and I realized that it would take three books to explain things clearly. With this new understanding I wrote rough outlines and started writing the first book of the three. By October, I had found my rhythm and was on my way. *The Light in 9/11: Shocked by Kindness, Healed by Love* was gestated over the next nine months only this time with much clearer understanding and direction.

Writing a book was an isolating experience. I needed long, unscheduled blocks of time to get into the flow of writing. But once in flow, the hours passed like minutes. I sat at my kitchen table those eighteen months and watched the seasons change, the days grow longer and shorter, and the wildlife walk in and out of my back yard. It was like heaven or hell, depending on the day, but something kept pushing me forward.

I bumped along through the fall and winter, dutifully writing to my outline each day. Even with the additional year, time was getting short. I began to understand why they say it takes two years to write a book.

I have continuously prayed for creative partnership with Cozmeena since its inception ten years ago. When I started this book those prayers were focused further trusting that the right people would show up. It may not be in the timing we hope for but they do always arrive and in perfect Divine Order.

One day in March 2018, as I was moving toward what I thought was the final draft, I was having an inspiring conversation with my new, like-minded, enlightened friend Ben Day. In an offhanded moment I asked Ben to read what I was working on. Without my asking, Ben took a swing at editing a chapter. What I got back was incredible. Here was this kind, calm, retired engineer from Bell Labs, graduate of Dartmouth class of 1966, and exactly the counsel and editor I had prayed for. Poof!

With incredible ease and grace, Ben showed up as my cocreator and skillful content editor. Ben's wisdom, patience, and understanding of my overall vision not only improved this book exponentially but also made it a fun, collaborative pleasure. With heartfelt love and respect, I call Ben my "Obi-Ben Kenobi" because he truly is my wise sage and counsel not to mention my dear, dear friend.

Because this book's purpose was always to be a stepping-stone to speaking, I knew I did not have time to go through the query process of sending out book proposals to agents and traditional publishers in the hopes of getting a contract. With the advent of the new independent publishing industry, it seemed only logical to go in this direction as I had always planned to create Cozmeena Enlightened Publishing as one of the avenues to bring the Cozmeena concept into the world.

I have had wonderful support from my friends near and far and my Cozmeena Community. Thank you to everyone who listened to me over the years, talking me off the ledge through the ups and downs, and discussing the nuances of Cozmeena, this book, and how to bring it all forward and into the future.

I am so grateful to Peggy Kafka Sackler—artist extraordinaire and direct descendant of Franz. One of the greatest gifts of this project was reconnecting and picking up where we left off twenty years ago. Peg's hand in drawing this beautiful cover, in chalk pastel, is exactly what I envisioned while writing this book and thinking about its cover. Peg's love for Teddy is reflected in the sunrise that dawns beside our beloved Twin Towers illuminating the beautiful future we can have by choosing to see the tragedy of 9/11 in a new light.

Peeka Tildesley for our lifelong friendship and morning chats that always give me a grounded start to my day.

Lillian Carroll, my soul sister, "big brain", and study partner for our afternoon chats about all things enlightened.

Terri Reinstein for our chats NJ to SC to remember how important old friends are regardless of distance.

Kristen Moebius Lassalette for our visionary brainstorming discussions to bring Cozmeena and its future products to the world.

Susan McDowell for your friendship, humor, patience, and candor after reading the first draft and the second draft.

Sean McDowell for thoughtful insights after wading through the second draft two times while having to relive your personal tragedies of 9/11.

Vicky LaVecchia for reading the first draft and telling me it was great even though it wasn't.

Despina Manatos for reading (and editing) the first draft and saying she was "riveted" which was especially meaningful coming from a high school English teacher.

Cindy and Ed Morea whose laughter and friendship got me through those long isolated months with biweekly dinners at Temple.

Jamie Turner for the many walks at Sandy Hook sharing your wisdom and guiding me through life and authorship. You are my chosen (older) sister.

My dear Kathy Vilardi—what can I say?

To Sarah Maris, my brilliant friend and webmaster, for her counsel and guidance in creating Cozmeena's on-line presence since its inception.

Kevin Ryan you make the world a better place, changing the lives of homeless teenagers every day. Your leadership and friendship is rare in this world. You personify kindness in everything you do both personally and professionally.

Sister Jenna for being our beautiful example of bringing love and light to the world through your work with American Meditating Radio and your visionary spiritual leadership through the Brahma Karmaris and the Meditation Museums in Washington, DC.

To the talented Paul Luftenegger whose song, "My Heart," along with other soulful, beautiful, *conscious music* compositions have soothed me and helped me to find my center through many difficult and anxious moments.

Elspeth Kerr, my spiritual cheerleader all the way from Cyprus, you reached out in perfect Divine Timing when I needed you most. Our Facebook conversations are the greatest example of the power and benefit of global social media!

Ingrid Vandervelt and the community of Empowering a Billion Women by 2020. You rock the world, iV! I am so grateful to have joined you and the remarkable women of EBW2020 for this incredible ride.

And to all the other sisters, brothers, spiritual leaders, and cocreators of the Brahma Karmari's at Peace Village including: Margaret Placentra Johnston, Andrea Pennington, Karena Virginia, Harriet Fulbright, Emily Hine, Rev Ivy Shadiah Hylton, Mali Phonpadith, Michele Shay, Kristin Hoffman, Ruby Lathan, Terrlyn Avery, Angela Holton, Skylar Liberty Rose, Valarie Alexander, Ivan Figueroa-Otero, and many others.

To my readers Paul Lyle, Jenny Portman, Bar Scott, Kathy Donnelly, Trude Dybendahl, Susan Kyrillos, Cathy Alescio, and Joe Liberi. I am indebted to you for your invaluable feedback that helped shape and hone this book.

To Nan Penman and Ron Honsa for filming and editing Voices of Inspiration.

Patty, Bobby, and Kat of Fair Haven's Tavalo Pronto whose smiling faces and warm, wonderful energy greets me each morning as I start my day (and my heart) with a cup of their delicious coffee.

To Val Barnaby and the Warrior Women of ESSA Sports Performance—Empowerment begins with a great leader, good friends, and challenging workouts.

Good Karma Café in Red Bank for sustaining me after many late nights of writing with your outrageous Love Bowls with tofu and peanut sauce.

Fair Haven Friends and River Road Books for being the warmest and most wonderful community I could ever ask for—our own Mayberry RFD in real time.

Beautiful Women of Cozmeena—my four hundred local and online knitters and friends extraordinaire. Thank you for your unending love, support, and encouragement via Facebook or in person. You kept me going on this project when I sometimes felt alone in the world.

My personal Facebook friends near and far, thank you for being my cheerleaders regarding this book and supporting Cozmeena Enlightened Living all these years. Our beautiful future awaits!

Dolores Hirschman for choosing me to share my message on your TEDx stage in New Bedford, Massachusetts, in November 2016. Your guidance in drafting my "idea worth sharing" was the first step in writing this book.

To Jen, Billy, and Timmy who have patiently tolerated my distracted, busy mind, listened to me talk about Cozmeena for the past ten years, and encouraged me with love and support as my awesome Team Luckett. Cozmeena may be my entertainment, purpose, and passion but you my dear, beautiful children, are my life's greatest work.

And to Teddy Luckett . . . my soul mate and greatest love. You loved me unconditionally. You made me better. I am honored to have known you at all.

For more information please visit www.cozmeena.com or www.lisaluckett.com

ABOUT THE AUTHOR

Lisa Luckett lives on the North Jersey Coast. When she isn't quoting movies and laughing with her young adult children, she is thinking about a better world and how to expand Cozmeena Enlightened Living.

Stacy Lyle Photography

Lisa Luckett is available for speaking engagements. Please contact her at www.lisaluckett.com

CPSIA information can be obtained
at www.ICGtesting.com
Printed in the USA
BVHW07s0713280718
522905BV00001B/1/P